A CHRISTMAS JOURNEY

A CHRISTMAS JOURNEY
Filled with Wonder, Marked by the Cross

DOUGLAS D. WEBSTER

CLEMENTS PUBLISHING
Toronto

Published 2007 by
Clements Publishing
213-6021 Yonge Street
Toronto, Ontario
M2M 3W2 Canada
www.clementspublishing.com

The author and publisher express special thanks to
Susan Montoya for her creative cover design,
Jim Meals for his editorial assistance,
and Alexis Pigott for her copy editing.

Webster, Douglas D.
A Christmas journey / Douglas D. Webster.

Includes bibliographical references.
ISBN-10: 1-894667-87-5
ISBN-13: 978-1-894667-87-6

1. Jesus Christ--Nativity. 2. Christmas. I. Title.

BT315.3.W42 2007   232.92
C2007-906193-1

CONTENTS

For
Dave and Kathie Jones
Hannah, Madison, Andy and Katie

a family
marked by the cross

PREFACE

Sooner or later we discover that home is not where we're from, but where we're going. We may come to this discovery as a rude awakening, because we tend to take home for granted, until we are out on our own and away from home. We thought the feeling of being at home was in the past, in our old neighborhood, but after a few return visits, we realize that it's no longer there. We thought it was in a place, among family and friends, but even there it seems missing. The Christmas season heightens this sense of loss. We would like to go back to how things used to be. But we can't get home on frequent flier miles and we can't resurrect missing family members. This is when we begin to realize that home is not where we're from, but where we're going. The quest for home is built into life. Nostalgia cannot fulfill this longing. Each of us has a story, but only one story redeems our story. The meaning of Christmas is all about that true story. Jesus left home to bring us home. The incarnation of God is the vital truth that makes coming home possible.

The best way to experience Christmas is to let the reality of the first Christmas fill our hearts and minds. We seek to focus on the truth of the Incarnation of God and celebrate the mystery and simplicity of that first Christ-centered Christmas. We want to be led in worship by the shepherds and the magi, the way they did it on that first Christmas Eve. Along with Mary and Joseph, we will worship better than we know. Out of relationships and circumstances, marred by pain and brokenness, we want to choose joy, not because we have will-power, but because we have the Savior. God's redeeming grace leads us home.

CHAPTER 1

WHAT IF JESUS NEVER CAME?

*"In him was life, and that life was the light of
all people. The light shines in the darkness,
and the darkness has not overcome it."*

John 1:4

"What if Jesus never came?" is best asked when life is thrown out of kilter, when our Christmas feels unsettled or disrupted, not because of the usual holiday activities, but because our souls have been touched or troubled in a significant way. As I look back, the Christmases that I remember being the most meaningful are the ones that were upsetting and disquieting. The Lord brings the message of Christmas home in unexpected and sometimes unsettling ways.

Sometimes our best laid plans for a merry Christmas don't go as expected. I remember one Christmas in Toronto, when all the preparations were completed—the gifts were wrapped, and the decorations were up. Our children were at a wonderful stage: Kennerly was two, Andrew five, and Jeremiah seven. It was much easier to impress them then than it is today. What made it even more exciting was that Grandma Webster was flying in from Chicago on Christmas Eve. She had a well-deserved reputation for being a great gift giver. Holiday traffic was heavy at the airport, so it took me longer to pick up my mother than we expected, but we finally arrived home. As we walked in the front door, we heard Kennerly screaming in pain. Minutes before, Kennerly had tripped while chasing her older brothers and had slammed head first into a door frame. She had a gash on her forehead that wouldn't stop bleeding and Virginia was trying to console her while pressing a towel against her forehead to stop the flow of blood. Since the cut was deep, we hurried off to the emergency room, leaving Andrew and Jeremiah with Grandma.

Apparently, Christmas Eve is a rough night for many families, because the ER was packed with people, many of whom were in far worse shape than Kennerly, although they weren't screaming like she was. We waited for three hours before a very tired doctor stitched up Kennerly's forehead, and I still remember holding my screaming two-year-old, who thought she was being tortured. Meanwhile, back at home, the boys had the situation completely under control. They had convinced Grandma that since they were so upset over Kennerly's accident, they should be able to open a gift. She agreed, but they ended up opening one gift every thirty minutes. We arrived home four hours later and the boys had opened all their gifts. They were thrilled! We were exhausted. That is the only time I remember sleeping in on Christmas morning.

Our minor set back on Christmas Eve is not meant to compete with the circumstances and difficulties you may be facing this Christmas. But it serves as a parable, reminding me that, try as we might, the real joy of Christmas lies outside our circumstances and all our preparations. If Jesus had never come, the measure of our lives would be what we make of it, and as plans go awry and preparations fail, life becomes a casualty of disappointments and frustrations. For as long as life rests on our own self effort and good fortune, the joy of life extends only to the happiness of our circumstances. Believing, as well as hearing, are best served by hard surfaces. Like a voice in a marble cathedral, the angel of the Lord's announcement, "Today in the town of David a Savior has been born to you; he is Christ the Lord" resonates best during hard Christmases (Luke 2:11). Dietrich Bonhoeffer, pastor and resistance fighter in Hitler's Germany, wrote to a friend from prison,

If I should still be kept in this hole over Christmas, don't worry about it. I'm not really anxious about it. One can keep Christmas as a Christian even in prison, more easily than family occasions, anyhow.[1]

SILENT NIGHT

By the time we get to Christmas Eve, we welcome the night. We're ready for candlelight at church and the soft glow of Christmas tree lights at home. We want sight and sound to be subdued and a sense of wonder to fill our hearts. Finally, we've come to the night before Christmas, "when all through the house not a creature was stirring, not even a mouse."

Who can forget Charles Moore's description of Santa? "His eyes—how they twinkled! His dimples how merry! His cheeks were like roses, his nose like a cherry!" We feel that childhood excitement around a brightly lit Christmas tree and see it in the eyes of a child opening her gifts. But that spark of nostalgia is not the lasting glory we truly seek. The holiday season hype subsides. The glow of Santa Claus fades: "I heard him exclaim, ere he drove out of sight, *Merry Christmas to all, and to all a good-night!*" There is something more serious, more sober at work here. Santa becomes a distraction; the Christ Child is our devotion. Our Savior's glory grows in grace and truth.

Our souls are ready for "Silent night! Holy night! All is calm, all is bright 'round yon virgin mother and Child, holy infant so tender and mild, sleep in heavenly peace, sleep in heavenly peace." This is the night we long for; the night of rest and peace, quiet joy and true worship. Restless energy cease! Hear the psalmist's call to worship, "Be still and know that I am God!"

On a dark night, away from city lights, the stars are illumined more vividly. Likewise, Rembrandt used the night to reveal the true light. His scenes of the Holy Nativity are shrouded in darkness in order to focus our attention on the one true light that was meant to give light to everyone in the world.

Rembrandt concentrated on depicting Mary and the baby Jesus in the years that his wife, Saskia, was giving birth to their children. Some believe that his wife and baby posed for his portraits and sketches of the Nativity. In a sensitive pen and ink wash Rembrandt shows Mary holding her newborn baby against her shoulder in an attitude of great tenderness and love. The sketch dates from 1635—the year their first child, a son named Rumbartus was born. Sadly, the little boy lived for only two months. For Rembrandt, his work was more than an exercise in religious art. It was an act of redemptive concentration. Rembrandt lost three of his four children in their early years of life. Only Titus, their fourth child, born in 1641 survived. In the darkness of his own grief he focused on the light and life of Christ.[2]

We welcome nightfall on Christmas Eve to quiet our hearts and focus our souls, but there is a second meaning to the metaphor of night that we are all well aware of. It is hinted at in the familiar Christmas carol, *"O little town of Bethlehem, how still we see thee lie! Above thy deep and dreamless sleep the silent stars go by. Yet in thy dark streets shineth the everlasting Light; the hopes and fears of all the years are met in thee tonight."* There is a night, a silent, holy night, that inspires devotion, but there is also a night that instills fear and dread. This is the night spoken of by the prophet Isaiah, when he wrote, "The people walking in darkness have seen a great light; on those living in the land of the shadow of death a light has dawned" (Isaiah 9:2). This is the night we describe as the dark night of the soul. When we feel we have no one to turn to and no hope to rest in. It is an overcoming darkness that descends upon us and fills us with dread and despair. This, too, is the Night before Christmas, the night of pain and loss, when we need the Light and Life of Christ. If the shepherds remind us of the silent, holy night of devotion and worship, King Herod reminds us of the dreaded night of death.

DARK NIGHT OF THE SOUL

Recently my Uncle Dave and Aunt Kathy Haumersen received a telephone call from a Diane Daly in Davenport, Iowa. Years ago they lived in Davenport, and the call came nearly twenty-five years to the day when Dave and Kathy's seven-year-old son, Chuckie, was hit by a car and killed as he stood several feet from the main entrance to his school. An impatient woman lost control of her car as she pulled away from the curb causing it to lurch forward and plow into Chuckie, killing him instantly. If his brother Steve had not gone back to close a neighbor's car door he would have been run over as well. The family was plunged into the darkest night they had ever experienced.

Dave and Kathy were just two weeks away from moving to Washington, D.C. where my uncle had accepted a job at the headquarters of the Corps of Engineers. They had sold their home and had purchased a great home for their family of five in a quiet D.C. suburb. As my uncle says, "We still left, but only four of us moved and the transition was very difficult—no church, no friends, but God still upheld us."

They arrived in Washington in time for Thanksgiving. Kathy remembers how small their little family seemed, just the four of them sitting at the Thanksgiving table in Alexandria. Dave asked the blessing and then had to excuse himself from the table when he finished praying. For the sake of Steve and Laura, just six and four years old, they had to keep going. In time, they felt the support of other believers. As Kathy explains, "The Lord graciously put us two doors away from a Christian family who had lost a five-year-old daughter five years prior to our moving to Virginia. Isn't it awesome how the Lord works things out? Our neighbors, Betty and Homer Hammersley, were aware of our situation because our realtor had told them. Betty was a very real help and comfort and cried right along with us. I'm sure we brought back a lot of difficult memories for them."

Before moving, Kathy sought out the woman who caused the accident. Kathy wanted her to know that "they held no grudge," and that while they didn't understand why this happened, they "knew the Lord was in control." One year after the fatal accident, my uncle and aunt placed a small picture of Chuckie and a short statement in the Davenport newspaper. It read:

In Memoriam: One year ago today our hearts were more than heavy because our son was taken from us . . . yet we rejoiced because his faith in Jesus brought him to a victorious heavenly homecoming that day. We would like to express our warmest thanks to our many Quad City friends for their expressions of love during that time. — *Dave & Kathy Haumersen*

Fast forward twenty-five years and the Haumesens receive a phone call from Diane Daly. She explains that she had read the newspaper piece and couldn't get over their confidence and peace. Diane had been so disturbed by the accident that she had trouble sleeping and eating for days afterwards. Her children were about Chuckie's age and attended the same elementary school. She knew that if she had dropped her children off just a few minutes earlier it might have been her son or daughter struck by the car. She asked herself how she would have responded if such a tragedy had struck her family. Diane was gripped by fear. Then, a year later, she read the note from Dave and Kathy in the paper. Diane knew she had to get what the Haumersens had—a peace that was beyond her understanding. She asked a friend, who she knew was a Christian, how she might experience this peace. One of the first things her friend did was to encourage her to attend a Bible study. She was impressed that the leader didn't pray from a prayer book. She had never heard such personal prayers, in communication with a loving God, or experienced such a down-to-earth Bible study. Diane was drawn to consider the claims of Christ in a fresh way. She came to the Lord and, over time, the rest of her family placed their trust in Christ.

Looking back, Diane sees clearly, "God taught me through that horrible incident to show me that my form of religion was so shallow that it couldn't withstand such a tragedy." She concluded our conversation by quoting a verse, "For God has not given us a spirit of fear, but of power and of love and of a sound mind" (1 Timothy 1:7 KJV). The only way home for Diane was through Christ.

Out of the darkness of Chuckie's tragic death the Light of Christ shined. "The people walking in darkness have seen a great light; on those living in the land of the shadow of death a light has dawned." The prophet

Isaiah found the source of this darkness-defeating Light in the coming of the child: "For to us a child is born, to us a son is given, and the government will be on his shoulders. And he will be called Wonderful Counselor, Mighty God, Everlasting Father, Prince of Peace" (Isaiah 9:2,6). The Light of Christ is not mood lighting for a traditional, child-centered Christmas. This is not the time to turn Christmas into special effects and spiritual themes. It is not the human spirit that is being celebrated, but the birth of the Incarnate One who lived and died and rose again that we might live an everlasting life.

The Lord graciously used the Haumersen's dark night of the soul in order to reveal the Light of Life. Their confidence in God's resurrection power and their reliance on the saving work of Christ, proved effective against the power of darkness. We can be thankful for this silent night, holy night, when all is calm, all is bright, for we know that the Light of Christ is powerful enough to overcome the darkest night—no matter how grave the evil.

To understand the power of the Light of Christ, we must move from the cradle to the cross. The wood of the manger reminds us of the wood of the Cross. Even at Christmas we are led from "Bethlehem's incarnation to Calvary's bitter cross," from the "Christmas Babe so tender" to the "Lamb who bore our blame." As Margaret Clarkson writes, "Joy to see You lying in your manger bed, weep to see You dying in our sinful stead. By Your birth so lowly, by Your love so true, By Your cross most holy, Lord, we worship You!"[3] The first great truth of Christmas is, "For unto us a child is born, unto us a son is given. . ." and the second unforgettable truth is, "For God so loved the world that he gave his one and only Son, that whoever believes in him shall not perish but have eternal life" (John 3:16).

GLORY NIGHT

We try hard to light up this season, but in spite of our extra efforts, nothing compares to the glory of the Lord. We're always trying to make this the best Christmas ever, but it never compares to the first

Christmas. That's how it should be. In Bill Keane's cartoon strip *Family Circus*, the kids are watching a commercial on television. A salesman, with outstretched arms proclaims, "Let's make this the Best Christmas EVER!" One of the kids responds, "Better than the FIRST one???" Keane drew above their heads a thought bubble depicting Mary and Joseph and the baby Jesus. In the far corner he shows the parents instinctively looking at one another, marveling at the wisdom of their daughter's comment.

If Jesus had never come, Zechariah would have carried out his religious duties and lived the rest of his days under the law. Elizabeth's life would have remained a very private story of disappointment and personal disgrace. Mary would have never sung her song of praise or lived her costly life of discipleship. Joseph would have continued to lead a simple life, uncomplicated by salvation history. The shepherds would have remained in the fields keeping watch over their flock by night. If Jesus had never come, there would have been no heavenly host singing, "Glory to God in the highest, and on earth peace to all upon whom his favor rests." The eastern magi would have had no star to follow, no run-in with Herod, no gifts to offer the newborn King. Simeon and Anna would have gone to their graves without seeing God's "salvation, prepared in the sight of all people, a light of revelation to the Gentiles and for glory to your people Israel."

Each person in the Christmas story shows us a dimension of life fulfilled because Jesus came. Like Zechariah, we are no longer under the law, but we can be saved by grace. Like Elizabeth, our private stories of pain and emptiness can be reversed because of the coming of the Lord. Like Mary, the Lord has been mindful of our humble state and the Mighty One has done great things for us, and that truth can change our lives. Because Jesus came, we have a song of praise to sing. Like Joseph, our simple lives can be caught up in something more powerful and redemptive than we ever imagined. Like the magi, we can follow the revelation of God until it leads us to the King and we bow and worship. And like Simeon and Anna, we can have faith to see the light of revelation and embrace the truth of Christ. Through the experience of those who celebrated the first Christmas, we see what we would be missing if Jesus had never come, and what can be ours if we receive this gift of God.

We remember the glory of the first Christmas, when "the glory of the Lord shone around them. . ." We long to celebrate the faith and promise of the first Christmas.

> Long my imprisoned spirit lay
> fast bound in sin and nature's night;
> Thine eye diffused a quickening ray,
> I woke, the dungeon flamed with light;
> my chains fell off, my heart was free;
> I rose, went forth and followed thee.
> Amazing love! How can it be
> that thou, my God,
> shouldst die for me?
> —Charles Wesley

CHAPTER 2

JESUS IS GOD

"For to us a child is born, to us a son is given, and the govern-
ment will be on his shoulders. And he will be called Wonderful
Counselor, Mighty God, Everlasting Father, Prince of Peace."
Isaiah 9:6

Michael Kelly of *The Washington Post* illustrates something far worse than the trivialization of Christmas in his article entitled, *"The white-light, colored-light debate."*[1] Since his wife is Jewish and he is Catholic they are raising their boys "to respect and love two great faiths that have a slight doctrinal disagreement between them." The boys like it because they receive presents for the eight days of Hanukkah *and* Christmas. According to their father, their "strong belief" is "the more gods the merrier." The Kellys have found the local Unitarian Church supportive because "Jesus Christ is celebrated as 'a very special person' and 'a great rabbi' and an all-around asset to the community." Michael Kelly is thankful that, "the Son-of-God debate, which has proved so regrettably contentious over the years," has been replaced by the white vs. colored lights debate.

For the followers of Jesus, everything depends on the true identity of Jesus the Christ as the Son of God and our relationship to him. Christmas is not about inspirational ideas that touch our lives in some vague, generic way. It is about the living Lord Jesus Christ who came to earth and put on our humanity, who lived and died and rose again. If it's not about him, specifically and personally, it's really not about anything at all.

Isaiah used four titles (Wonderful Counselor, Mighty God, Everlasting Father and Prince of Peace) to explain and expound on the meaning of Immanuel, God with us. The prophet makes it impossible to evade the claim that God himself had come. The titles clearly affirm what the apostle confessed: "For God was pleased to have all his fullness dwell in him, and through him to reconcile to himself all things" (Colossians 1:19). The titles attributed to this child by Isaiah remind us of what the author of Hebrews wrote, "The Son is the radiance of God's glory and the exact representation of his being, sustaining all things by his powerful word" (Hebrews 1:3). The witness of the prophets and the apostles agree, and Christians unequivocally confess that Jesus is the Wonderful Counselor, the Mighty God, the Everlasting Father and the Prince of Peace.

THE HOLY FAMILY

Of all four titles, the boldest one may be Everlasting Father, especially for those who believe in God the Father, Son and Holy Spirit. There is at least an initial pause sparked by that title that calls for serious reflection. The title does not mean that all of God lies in the manger, or that all of God hangs on the Cross, but it does mean that the child who was laid in a manger, and who would one day die on the cross, was fully God and fully human. *There is absolutely nothing about God's being, character and work, that can not be said of this child who is born for us.*

What the prophet Isaiah affirmed in the title, Everlasting Father, is profoundly explored in the Gospel of John. The prologue addresses the essential relationship between Jesus and the Father: "The Word became flesh and made his dwelling among us. We have seen his glory, the glory of the One and Only, who came from the Father, full of grace and truth" (John 1:14). The Son's authority could not be greater: "The Father loves the Son and has placed everything in his hands" (John 3:35). And to worship the Father in spirit and in truth was to accept Jesus as the Messiah (John 4:23-26). All the activity of Jesus was consistent with and dependent upon the work of the Father. As Jesus said, "My Father is always at his work to this very day, and I, too, am working" (John 5:17).

By "calling God his own Father," Jesus made "himself equal with God," and raised the violent objection of the religious authorities (John 5:18). However, he insisted that the Son, "can do nothing by himself; he can do only what he sees his Father doing, because whatever the Father does the Son also does" (John 5:19). Once again, the motivation for this work is love: "For the Father loves the Son and shows him all he does" (John 5:20). And the life and death power of the Son is consistent with the Father's work (John 5:22,26). Jesus saw himself executing the Father's will and receiving the honor due to the Father: "He who does not honor the Son does not honor the Father, who sent him" (John 5:23). To know the Father is to know the Son and to know the Son is to know the Father (John 6:46; 8:19).

Tradition marks Christmas as a special family time, but the center of the celebration is not your family or mine. "The true 'holy family' in the Bible is not Mary, Joseph, and their baby; it is the Father, the Son, and the Holy Spirit."[5] The sentiment of the season may focus on precious children and a mother's tender love, but the reason for the celebration is that God in three persons—Father, Son, and Holy Spirit—exists in perfect community and complete fellowship. And within this holy family there is no longing for fulfillment, or feeling of vulnerability, or yearning for love, or striving for significance. There is nothing lacking that needs completion, or corrupt that needs fixing. No one could ever add to the glory and love that characterized the Holy Family, and everything that issues from this perfect relationship is motivated by love. It is God's Love alone, the divine necessity, that led first to Creation and then to Redemption by way of the Cross.

By centering on the true holy family, we begin to ease the pressure that builds during the holidays, the burden that often leaves us stressed out, melancholy, and blue. If we make Christmas all about what we do for others and what others do for us, it is no wonder that we're left feeling hassled and disappointed. The gift of Christ deserves far more of our attention than just a few moments of quiet reflection on Christmas Eve.

The title Everlasting Father points us beyond ourselves to the one who called us into being, not to fill his needs, but to lovingly meet our needs. Human love can be such a mixed blessing with its conflicted motives and strange illusions, that it is difficult for us to grasp the beauty and goodness of Divine Love. But God's love seeks only to make it possible for us to respond to his love, a love that exceeds all that we could ever ask for or imagine.

ADVENT LOVE

The paradox could not be more striking: the baby in the manger is the Eternal Father. But in order to give this paradox the meaning intended by Isaiah, we must remove from the title Eternal Father any notion of biological generation and gender designation. The meaning of "Father" has nothing to do with conception or patriarchy. It is a relational description that underscores the love of God. All that can possibly be conveyed by divine love lies behind the designation of Everlasting Father. Just as all the wisdom and comfort of the Wonderful Counselor is to be attributed to this child, as well as all the power and holiness of the Mighty God, so it is only right to attribute all the love of the Everlasting Father to this child. This love includes, even transcends everything that is meant by familial love, maternal love, and parental love. All that can possibly be said about God's love for us lies behind this designation, and it draws out our dependency upon our Heavenly Father's love.

The Psalms portray the significance of this title by placing the transcendent majesty of God side-by-side with the immediacy of God's fatherly love: "Sing to God, sing praise to his name, extol him who rides on the clouds—his name is the Lord—and rejoice before him. A father to the fatherless, a defender of widows, is God in his holy dwelling. God sets the lonely in families . . ." (Psalm 68:4-6). King David linked the Father's love to our weakness and frailty. "As a father has compassion on his children, so the Lord has compassion on those who fear him; for he knows how we are formed, he remembers we are dust. As for man, his days are like grass, he flourishes like a flower of the field; the wind blows over it and it is gone, and its place remembers it no more. But from everlasting to everlasting the Lord's love is with those who fear him, and his righteousness with their children's children—with those who keep his covenant and remember to obey his precepts" (Psalm 103:13-18).

The title Everlasting Father underscores not only the deep mystery of the triune character of God but it emphasizes our total dependence upon the Father's love. In a name it points to the perfect relationship within the Godhead and at the same time our orphaned status apart from the Father. We need the Father's love and we need it forever. No matter how greatly we are loved by family and friends, apart from God's love, we are as good as unloved. And no matter how unloved we consider ourselves to be, in Christ we are greatly loved! All other loves are transitory and undependable and need the love of God to be sustained. Even the deepest bond between husband and wife, or parent and child, proves inadequate apart from the love of the Everlasting Father.

Unlike Advent power, which is the power of God to transcend his majesty and glory, Advent love is the most immediate and personal revelation of God's love. His power may have been hidden in secret visions, in a miraculous conception, and in fulfilled prophecy, but his love was revealed in deeply personal ways. Zechariah and Elizabeth's prayers were answered and her barrenness removed. Joseph's painful resignation gave way to joy and Mary's "humble state" turned to blessing and praise. God drew them into his great redemptive purpose, and at the same time lovingly met their personal needs for assurance, significance, and fulfillment. The harmony between God's holy will and true personal fulfillment was evident at Advent and remains true today. The love of the Everlasting Father does not destroy the person to save his or her soul, but fulfills the person to save the world. "For God so loved the world that he gave his one and only Son," and in the giving takes nothing away except sin and death!

ADOPTED CHILDREN

In the Gospel of John, Jesus worked out what it meant for the Son to bear the authority, power, glory, love, and will of the Father. Isaiah's prophecy rightly entitled the child who was born the Everlasting Father, and through the Gospel of John we gain a deeper understanding of this great truth. But Jesus took it even further. Not only did he declare, "I am in my Father," but he said to all who believed in him, "you are in me, and I am in you" (John 14:20). "If anyone loves me," Jesus said, "he will obey my teaching. My Father will love him, and we will come to him and make our home with him" (John 14:23).

Jesus made a startling statement about our family relationship. After he explained that he was the good shepherd who lays his life down for the sheep (John 10:15), he said, "The reason my Father loves me is that I lay down my life—only to take it up again" (John 10:17). That is not to say that the only reason the Father loved him was because he gave up his life on the Cross, but it shows just how significant our place in the family is and how great God's love for us is. A second startling statement joins together the unity of the Household of Faith, the unity of the Godhead and the testimony to the world that the Father sent the Son. Jesus prayed for all believers, "that all of them may be one, Father, just as you are in me and I am in you. May they also be in us, so that the world may believe that you have sent me" (John 17:21). Think of it! Jesus expected the unity of the body of Christ to bear witness to the world of his true identity.

The Christmas message brings us to our knees and causes us to thank the Lord for his indescribable Gift. We worship as Paul worshiped and we pray as he prayed: "For this reason I kneel before the Father, from whom his whole family in heaven and on earth derives its name. I pray that out of his glorious riches he may strengthen you with power through his Spirit in your inner being, so that Christ may dwell in your hearts through faith" (Ephesians 3:14-17). We are not fatherless, cosmic orphans, estranged from the most meaningful relationship possible, but in Christ we are the true sons and daughters of God. Bernard of Clairvaux was right when he said, "We should love God because he is God, and the measure of our love should be to love him without measure."

CHAPTER 3

A CHRISTIAN CHRISTMAS

*"This will be a sign to you: You will find a baby
wrapped in strips of cloth and lying in a manger."*
Luke 2:12

In the fourth century the church chose to celebrate the birth of Christ on December 25, the start of the Winter Solstice. The church took over this particular day because it was designated as the Natal Day of the Unconquerable Sun by the Persian religion of Mithraism. Christians sought to replace the old heathen festival with the celebration of the "Son of Righteousness." Increase Mather of Boston wrote in 1687 that early Christians observed Christ's Nativity on December 25 not "thinking that Christ was born in that month, but because the Heathens Saturnalia was at the time kept in Rome, and they were willing to have those Pagan Holidays metamorphosed into Christian ones." Christmas was an alternative to the Feast of Saturn, which under the Roman Caesar Caligula lasted five days and was known for public drunkenness and revelry.

The Puritans wanted nothing to do with Christmas. They saw it as a combination of our modern day Halloween and Mardi Gras, an excuse for excess and indulgence. Cotton Mather wrote in 1712: "The Feast of Christ's Nativity is spent in Reveling, Dicing, Carding, Masking, and in all Licentious Liberty . . . by Mad Mirth, by long Eating, by hard Drinking, by lewd Gaming, by rude Reveling . . .["6] The custom of Mumming, which involved "changing clothes between men and women to make merry in disguise," was part of the Christmas ritual. As was the ritual of social inversion: "Christmas was a time when peasants, servants, and apprentices exercise the right to demand that their wealthier neighbors and patrons treat them as if they were wealthy and powerful."[7] For many it was an excuse to go wassailing, or drinking. Stephen Nissenbaum writes, "It may not be going too far to say that Christmas has always been an extremely difficult holiday to Christianize. Little wonder that the Puritans were willing to save themselves the trouble."[8]

Nissenbaum contends that religion failed to "transform Christmas from a season of misrule into an occasion of quieter pleasure . . . The 'house of ale' would not be vanquished by the house of God, but by a new faith that was just beginning to sweep over American society. It was the religion of domesticity, which would be represented at Christmas-time not by Jesus of Nazareth but by a newer and more worldly deity—Santa Claus."[9]

The traditional Christmas we now celebrate was largely invented in the 19th Century. The familiar Santa Claus story appears to have been devised in the early 19th Century. Over time, Christmas became more of a child-centered event, and thus modified the earlier ritual of social inversion. Clement Moore and Washington Irving, high church Episcopalians who were politically conservative and part of the upper-class New York City aristocracy, promoted the more popular, secular version of Christmas. In 1822 Moore wrote "A Visit from Saint Nicholas." The first pictures of Santa Claus appeared around 1848. He was still a small, thin, elf-like creature in 1863 who could fit down a chimney, but by 1881 he had grown to be a jolly, red-suited, white bearded Santa. In time, the rowdier elements of Christmas disappeared, and in their place was a domestic and child-centered Christmas.

By the mid-1820's Santa Claus was beginning to sell commercially produced Christmas presents and by the 1840's he had become a commercial icon. He was projected as a figure of great antiquity, permitting "the holiday gift exchange [to be] rooted in something deeper and more 'authentic' than the dynamics of the marketplace."[10] Santa mythologized consumption. As Stephen Nissenbaum explains, "Consumerism was coming to supplant chaos as the new problem of the holiday season. The battle for Christmas was beginning to change from physical struggle that pitted the classes against one another into a moral one that divided the generations."[11]

Christmas trees became widely known in the US during the mid-1830's. On Christmas Eve young children were surprised by a tree illuminated by open candles. These trees were often more like centerpieces than our free-standing 7' fir trees. They were the tops of an evergreen tree that were set up in rooms which were off limits to children until that special moment on Christmas Eve.

It takes me just about 12 months to forget how much work is involved in decorating the house for Christmas. We haul out our boxes of Christmas decorations from the garage. We buy a tree, set it up, and string it with lights. Some years we get a great tree, but other years, what looked good on the Christmas tree lot doesn't look so good in our living room. We've found the poorer the tree the more crucial the placement of lights and ornaments.

I remember one year, when I was in junior high, we got a really poor tree. There was a gaping hole in it that we didn't notice when we bought it, partly because we were freezing in sub-zero temperatures. This was when I was growing up in Buffalo, New York. My mother solved the problem by putting a whole cut-out manger scene in the blank spot. Family and friends who visited commented on our creativity.

This past year we got a good tree. Virginia and Andrew picked it out, and the best part of all was that Andrew put it up. I came home and there it was, all set up, and Virginia had strung the lights. All I did was put up some ornaments with Kennerly. Many of our ornaments bring back memories of when our children were young. Some of them were handmade in first grade. Red and green candles are used for the table centerpiece and a manger scene is placed on the tea table. We put on Christmas music and bake Christmas cookies, the kind that you frost with brightly colored icing. This is how we get in the mood, because this is how we've gotten in the mood for years. Of course, the malls go to extremes to create a holiday feeling in order to increase sales. Elaborate decorations are everywhere. It's as if an army of Santas descended to gift wrap an entire season in candy-cane red and string-up Christmas lights everywhere.

My mother remembers celebrating Christmas in typical Norman Rockwell fashion. She sat on the knee of the department store Santa Claus and shared her personal wish-list. She never questioned how he could be in so many stores at the same time, because she remembered being told that God was everywhere. If God could be everywhere, then Santa could be, too. It helped her to know that Santa flew around on a sleigh pulled by flying reindeer. But then one Christmas Eve she had a rude awakening. Every year her family gathered together with all the aunts and uncles and cousins at their grandparents' home.

This was a big house with four fireplaces, a grand stairway leading to the second floor, and a back stairway leading to servants' quarters on the third floor. My mother remembers the butler's pantry with floor to ceiling mahogany cupboards, and the dark paneled chauffeur's side entrance, with the marble washbasin in the secret bathroom. When they could get away with it, the cousins liked playing with the built-in dumb waiter—the pulley-drawn elevator that carried trays from the kitchen to the second floor. On that particular Christmas Eve one of my mother's cousins climbed in for a ride and got stuck between floors. His cries for help brought the adults running from downstairs. Of course, in their panic they scolded the innocent children who had nothing to do with their cousin getting stuck, while they comforted the delinquent and made him a hero upon his release.

As in previous years, the adults gathered the children into the large living room on Christmas Eve to anxiously await the coming of Santa Claus. The tension was almost unbearable. Suddenly they heard the telltale "ho-ho-ho-Merry Christmas" and there he was, peering into the room through one of the great long windows. He carried a huge sack of gifts over his shoulder. Like every other Christmas Eve, my mother was awestruck—but then something very disturbing happened. She overheard her oldest sister, Jeanne, say to her second oldest sister, Carol, "It's Uncle Connie!" My mother gasped at the outrageous thought, but her sister, with an air of confidence, whispered in a matter-of-fact tone, "There never was a real Santa Claus. It's always one of our uncles dressed up to look like Santa for the little kids." My mother was crushed and immediately began to argue with Jeanne. But she just grinned and said softly, "Do you see Uncle Connie here?"

After Jeanne's well-timed observation, no Santa costume could disguise Uncle Connie. My mother's belief in Santa was shattered. As soon as they got home, she verified the hoax by asking her mother. And in true parental fashion, my grandmother proceeded to scold her truth-telling daughter: "Jeanne, I'm so disappointed in you." Jeanne's Christmas Eve was ruined, but not as much as my mother's. There was no Santa Claus! She remembered all those times that she had shared her wish-list with the department store Santa and carefully laid out cookies and hot chocolate for Santa. She felt humiliated by the very thought. She wondered what else wasn't true, and Jeanne was only too happy to tell her about the tooth fairy.

The magic of the season is at odds with the mystery of Christmas, and the myth of Santa Claus contradicts the meaning of Jesus. There's a lot that goes on that Jesus doesn't deserve or want credit for. The mall and the manger clash. Judging from the Christmas specials on TV and the holiday frenzy at the malls, Jesus isn't the reason for the season, at least not for the secular season. What does Christ in the manger have to do with the shopper in the mall? Is there a way to get from the child-centered consumer Christmas to the Christ-centered contemplative Christmas?

I like Christmas trees and all the decorations that surround this season, but I love even more the symbols and signs of the first Christmas. There's no comparison between the terrified shepherds confronted by the glory of the Lord and modern shoppers. Holiday cheer is no match for the "good news of great joy that will be for all the people" (Luke 2:10). Nor can the Christmas specials be compared to the heavenly host proclaiming, "Glory to God in the highest, and on earth peace to all men and women who please him" (Luke 2:14). God didn't bring anything out of storage to decorate the scene, but the heavens opened and the angels sang.

Amidst all the ads, promotions, and Christmas cards, only one announcement really matters, "Today in the town of David a Savior has been born to you; he is Christ the Lord" (Luke 2:12). And at the center of this first Christmas, we find a manger, a wooden feed trough, used to cradle Jesus. It would be hard to find a symbol more earthy than the manger, which bore no sentimental value and evoked no nostalgic feelings. When Luke quoted the angelic announcement, "This will be a sign to you: You will find a baby wrapped in strips of cloth and lying in a manger," he introduced a powerful metaphor for God's self-imposed, sacrificial powerlessness (Luke 2:12). In this divinely appointed object lesson, the manger becomes a profound illustration of the humility of God. It is a radical picture of God's self-emptying. God himself, in the man Christ Jesus, condescends to join our helpless state in order to redeem us and restore us to right relationship with himself. Like the cross, the manger illustrates the extent of Christ's love.

Mass market commercialization has surrounded every Christmas we can remember, but there is a material existence that defies the world's materialism. God's very own radical material reality lay in a manger. The Incarnation is the grand miracle of the Christian Faith. God himself materialized in flesh and blood. "The Word became flesh and lived for a while among us. We have seen his glory, the glory of the one and only Son, who came from the Father, full of grace and truth." This is what the early Christians in the fourth century celebrated in the creeds. They proclaimed, "We all unanimously teach that we should confess that our Lord Jesus Christ is one and the same Son, truly God and truly man, one with the Father in his deity and one with us in our humanity, like us in all things except sin." This Incarnate One, lying in a manger, is the fact proclaimed by faith, against all fantasies and ideologies. Here is the mystery that defies magic and myth. Herein lies the true reason for this Holy Season.

However, if we're not careful, we can twist the message of Christ's manger and use it to "baby" our faith. The meaning of the manger can be transposed from a symbol of surrender and humility into a seasonal symbol generating feelings of warmth and tenderness. The manger can be used nostalgically to symbolize maternal love instead of Christ's sacrifice; it can be used sentimentally to symbolize the gift of babies instead of the gift of Salvation. How we invoke the biblical image of the manger determines whether we use or abuse this symbol. If Christ and his Word shape the meaning of the manger, then God's visual aid will retain its effectiveness in shaping our discipleship.

Our aim must be to understand the biblical sign of the manger in the light of God's salvation history and apply its message in a way that strengthens and inspires our faithfulness to Christ. It was a sign of humility that was meant to confirm reality. The setting was special by being decidedly indecorous, plain and simple. Nothing was allowed to distract from the wonder of the birth. It was not the birth of babies in general that inspired the shepherds' awe, but the birth of this particular baby. All significance was attributed to this singular truth—this particular Person. At the center of this scene was not a glorious abstraction, a general symbol for celebrating life, but the living Lord Jesus, Immanuel, God with us, the One to be worshiped as the Way, the Truth, and the Life.

JESUS UNEMBELLISHED

Jesus entered the world with nothing. The first Christmas was intentionally simple. The picture we have of the manger is uncluttered by explanation and tradition. There is no ornamentation or decoration. The story is as austere as the setting. The call to worship came to shepherds in a cathedral not made by human hands. Its dark sky canopy above and rocky terrain below were perfect for the sights and sounds of revelation. Who better than shepherds, their eyes accustomed to the dark and their ears alert to predators, to hear the terse announcement from the angel of the Lord, "Do not be afraid. I bring you good news of great joy that will be for all the people. Today in the town of David a Savior has been born to you; he is Christ the Lord. This will be a sign to you: You will find a baby wrapped in strips of cloth and lying in a manger" (Luke 2:10-12).

Once again, Rembrandt understood the meaning of Christmas. He was sensitive to this austerity in his paintings. All is calm in his earthy nativity scenes. All is dark, except for a brilliant light that emanates from a source hidden from our view. It is as if the light comes from the Christ child and illuminates the expressions of awe and wonder on the faces of Mary and Joseph, and the shepherds. At Christmas we long for that which Rembrandt captured in his paintings of the manger: Jesus unembellished. Jesus free from religious trappings, holiday hype, sentimentality and nostalgia. There is a difference between elaborating on the meaning of the Incarnation and embellishing the Christmas story. God chose the simplest of settings in which to reveal the Savior. There was nothing there to speak of but Christ. God wanted this awesome austerity impressed upon our souls. As Jesus emptied himself, God emptied the nativity of all but Jesus.

The God-intended austerity of Christ in the manger challenges our faith. Why do we long for something more than Jesus? Is our faith so weak that the mystery of the Incarnation is insufficient to hold our attention? We seem eager to fill the emptiness with ritual, tradition, and homey lessons. Are we unaware that God *designed* the stark simplicity of the manger to highlight the truth of the Incarnation?

We come closest to celebrating the true meaning of Christmas when, in the providence of God, we experience hardship and loss at Christmas. It may be the loss of a loved one, or a life-threatening illness, or a family crisis, but whatever it is, it forces us to seek a truer and more lasting comfort than the familiar rituals. Holiday cheer only serves to mock our grief and intensify our suffering. The festive sights and sounds of the season are no match for the stark realities of our lives. All the color is drained out of our holiday picture, and we seem to be left in the dark. Only then, when our lives are swept clean of all diversions and distractions, that our devotion to Christ can grow. Everything else is in the shadows, but the light of Christ shines in our lives. We become impressed with one overwhelming, awesome truth: Jesus is our Savior.

Joni Eareckson Tada is paralyzed from the neck down. She recalls one Christmas Eve when she felt like a failure. Everything around her was perfect. The candlelight sanctuary was beautiful and she was surrounded by a worshiping congregation, but inside she had no feelings for adoration and praise. "Then the bittersweet strains of a familiar carol reached her heart. *O come, O come Emmanuel, and ransom captive Israel that mourns in lonely exile here.* This described her feelings exactly. *O come, Thou Dayspring, come and cheer our spirits by Thine advent here. Disperse the gloomy clouds of night, and death's dark shadows put to flight.* In the depths of her soul, Joni cried out, 'That's how I feel!' Then she bowed her head and asked the Lord to take away her gloom and bring her joy. And he did." Jill Briscoe concludes her story about Joni with this wise counsel: "Whether it's disobedience, disappointment, disability, or whatever . . . . Jesus comes to dawn on every form of darkness . . . Is your Christmas this year a bleak one? Concentrate on that first beam—the Christ child in the manger. Sit still with the God who sends the dawn, and watch all that this Christ-light will transform in your life."[12]

To be honest, Jesus isn't the reason for much of what we do this season. If adults get so confused, what hope is there for children? Can we blame them for thinking Santa is the reason for the season? We can begin to make the difference between a child-centered, consumer Christmas and a Christ-centered, contemplative Christmas by distinguishing between the decorative symbols for the holiday season and the devotional symbols that lead us to worship our Savior, Jesus Christ. The manger is a good place to begin, because it is the antithesis of all the holiday hype. "This will be a sign to you: You will find a baby wrapped in strips of cloth and lying in a manger" (Luke 2:12). God chose the humility of the manger to display the grand miracle of the Incarnation. The myth of Santa Claus helps hide and excuse excessive marketing and materialism, but the mystery of the Incarnation reveals Jesus Christ, truly God and truly man.

The manger is also an important symbol for how we represent the Gospel of Christ today. It is easy to see from this simple visual aid that God entered into the experience of our humanity fully, but it may not be as easy to apply the meaning of the manger to the followers of Jesus. Do we entertain the notion that God seeks to advance the gospel through our prominence and worldly success? Do we feel pressured to compete against the marketplace in order to spread the good news? God's message of the manger strongly implies otherwise. The humility of the manger led to the humility of the Cross in order that the world might be saved through Christ. The manger brings the message of Christmas home, even as we are brought home to Christ.

CHAPTER 4

THE PRINCE OF PEACE

"Peace I leave with you; my peace I give you. I do
not give to you as the world gives. Do not let your
hearts be troubled and do not be afraid."

John 14:27

We long for peace, but if there is anything that tends to be in short supply during the holiday season, it is peace. My Aunt Jeanne, who is getting on in years, decided to host a large Christmas luncheon for her friends, so she called Aunt Carol, who is also getting on in years, and asked if she would help her put on the luncheon.

"No, I'm sorry," said Aunt Carol, "I couldn't possibly do anything more. I already have so much to do and I haven't even gotten to my cards." There was a pause at the other end of the line.

"I'm so disappointed in you," said Aunt Jeanne, "because I can't do it alone." She had, of course, already invited everyone and was beginning to feel overwhelmed with the prospect of putting on a Christmas luncheon by herself. So, a few hours later, Aunt Jeanne's fifty-five year old son called Aunt Carol to let her know how disappointed he was that she couldn't help his mother. "Couldn't you possibly honor my mother by helping her this way, for after all she is your sister."

Aunt Carol repeated, "I'm sorry, I just can't. I have so much on and I haven't even started my cards." By now, news of Aunt Carol being such a disappointment was spreading. In the course of the afternoon she received phone calls from three of Aunt Jeanne's friends who couldn't understand why Aunt Carol couldn't help her sister. So Carol did what all good sisters do and called her other sister, my mother who lived 1500 miles away. "Lou, I feel like such a failure. I'm disappointing everyone, and all I'm trying to do is get ready for Christmas." Thankfully, the whole episode was shortly put to rest. Aunt Jeanne couldn't find her glasses, which rendered her helpless and prompted her to call everyone on her list to cancel the luncheon. We were left to speculate that probably my uncle Merrill had, in his wise and quiet way, hidden her glasses to put an end to the problem of the Christmas luncheon.

SEARCH FOR PEACE

This story pokes fun at what we do to ourselves during the holiday season, but there is a much more serious side to consider. Especially at this time of year, we have a heightened sensitivity to the need for peace. We long for peace, a real peace that will put our hearts at rest.

What do I say to the dear woman whose husband of 28 years abandoned her just before Christmas? A year later, on the anniversary of his departure, he wrote,

> I know that my leaving the marriage was a great shock and a
> terrible blow to you. . . . It gives me anguish to know that my
> leaving caused you pain; yet I can only hope that, having passed
> through that pain, you will arrive at a more fulfilled, peaceful
> and joyful place in your life. . .Christmas has always been a very
> nostalgic and beautiful time to me, and I will always remember
> the fun times we had with the holidays in the early years of our
> marriage. . .I wish you well during this festive season, and for
> the new year to come. As time progresses, I hope that you will
> find new direction and fulfillment in your life, and that we can

respect and acknowledge one another for who we are. Merry Christmas.

The truth is that because of Christ she has come to a place of peace and fulfillment, but no thanks to the husband who left her.

The peace we long for involves many concerns, such as health, prosperity, well-being, security, the absence of war, and a release from anxiety. It can be peace of mind, goodwill and harmony with others, personal contentment, and freedom from persecution. But above all else, we long for peace with God, even if we can't identify the longing. As Augustine said in his *Confessions*, "Our hearts are restless until they find their rest in you." If one word captures the essence of salvation it is the Hebrew word, *shalom*, which means completeness, soundness, and wholeness. To be at peace is to be whole, to be at rest in our souls and fulfilled in our lives.

Shalom embraces the fullness of salvation, which means deliverance from "sin and death; guilt and estrangement; ignorance of truth; bondage to habit and vice; fear of demons, of death, of life, of God, of hell; despair of self; alienation from others; pressures of the world; a meaningless life." The meaning of Shalom is exceedingly positive, embracing "peace with God, access to God's favor and presence, hope of regaining the glory intended for humankind, endurance in suffering, steadfast character, an optimistic mind, inner motivations of divine love and power of the Spirit, ongoing experience of the risen Christ and sustaining joy in God."[13]

We have to admit that we are incapable of establishing this peace for ourselves. We cannot create *shalom*, any more than we can save ourselves. We are poor candidates for peace—our bodies break down, people fail us, terrorists attack, friends betray us, and war breaks out. Where is the peace we long for?

The world's strategies for obtaining peace have not been very successful. When President Bush confidently declares that the United States of America will lead the world to peace, we know we cannot deliver. When "Winston Churchill lay critically ill, he reflected on conditions in the world he had so heroically helped rescue. 'There is no hope,' he sighed. 'There is no hope.' And with that despairing observation, the great leader died," but the question survives: "Is there no hope? Were Churchill's dying words the epitaph for our age?"[14]

Understandably, one of the key words for Christmas is *Peace*. What is not so readily recognized is that Peace depends on the one who is called the Prince of Peace. Of course, to some, Christmas would be easier to celebrate if they just concentrated on the sentimental mood of Christmas and ignored its meaning. Tradition works fairly well without Truth, and fantasy is probably easier to accept than faith in the Lord Jesus Christ. Exchanging gifts can be done without thinking about the indescribable gift of God's own Son, and in the interests of good taste and tolerance, we could simply say, "Peace on earth," and leave it at that. Then everyone could get on with their "happy holidays."

In Isaiah's prophecy of Christ, the four titles culminate in the promise of peace. The wisdom of the Wonderful Counselor, the power of the Mighty God and love of the Everlasting Father leads to an enduring peace. The impact of God's work on our behalf, his comforting wisdom, his empowering might, and his everlasting love, provides a lasting peace. Of the four names given to this child who was to be born, the title Prince of Peace seems the most down-to-earth and the most human. Even the title appears to bear a more human designation than divine. Instead of calling this child King of kings and Lord of lords, which Handel's Hallelujah Chorus and the three preceding titles suggest, the title Prince of Peace emphasizes his humanity. It calls attention to the one who will not only establish peace, but embody peace. The Prince of Peace is himself a whole person, "the perfectly integrated, rounded personality, at one with God and humankind, but also a Prince," who administers all these benefits to his people.[15]

Since 9/11 and the war on terrorism, peace is on everyone's mind, but the peace we are looking for seems to be a multi-faith message of peace and tolerance. Anything that hints at a singular truth that people might find offensive or exclusionary causes many to object. Muslim extremists have done more to advance the secular cause of generic peace and tolerance than the ACLU could have ever dreamed possible. Christmas became harder when a wedge was driven between the promise of peace and the Prince of Peace. It is one thing to take the nativity scene out of the public square, it is quite another to eliminate Jesus Christ, the Prince of Peace, from the meaning of Christmas. Sincerity has replaced the Savior in a world that hopes to achieve peace through pluralism. What the prophet Jeremiah said about his day applies to our own: "They dress the wound of my people as though it were not serious. 'Peace, peace,' they say, when there is no peace" (Jeremiah 6:14, see Ezekiel 13:16; 1 Thessalonians 5:3).

ADVENT PEACE

In these troubled times, we are reminded of the promise of peace and who it is that fulfills the promise—the Prince of Peace. The announcement to the shepherds is not just a good line in an old story; it is the truth that shapes the course of history.

> Suddenly a great company of the heavenly host appeared with the angel, praising God and saying, 'Glory to God in the highest, and on earth peace to all on whom his favor rests.'

"Peace on earth" minus the Prince of Peace is really no peace at all, but an empty slogan. True peace requires the fullness of the angelic greeting: God's glory in the highest cannot be subtracted and God's favor cannot be forgotten. God's Shalom is not imposed, it is bestowed; it is not earned, it is given; it is not achieved, it is received. The peace we long for is not something we can give to ourselves. It is not dependent upon our circumstances, or our health, or on those around us. Advent Peace is not achieved through military might or romantic love or material success. It is achieved by the Prince of Peace, whose task it was "to reconcile to himself all things, whether things on earth or things in heaven, by making peace through his blood, shed on the cross" (Colossians 1:20).

Shalom is the gift of God that is based on a personal relationship with Jesus Christ, who paid the price for our peace. Isaiah's prophecy moves us from the exalted titles to the humble sacrifice, from the manger to the Cross: "Surely he took up our infirmities and carried our sorrows, yet we considered him stricken by God, smitten by him, and afflicted. But he was pierced for our transgressions, he was crushed for our iniquities; the punishment that brought us peace was upon him, and by his wounds we are healed" (Isaiah 53:4-5). Because of Christ's sacrifice, the apostle Paul was able to write, "Therefore, since we have been justified through faith, we have peace with God through our Lord Jesus Christ. . ." (Romans 5:1). Simeon foresaw the price of peace when he held the baby Jesus in his arms and said to Mary, "This child is destined to cause the falling and rising of many in Israel, and to be a sign that will be spoken against, so that the thoughts of many hearts will be revealed. And a sword will pierce your own soul too" (Luke 2:34-35).

Jesus knew that the gift of peace would be scorned by many. This is why he said, "Do not suppose that I have come to bring peace to the earth. I did not come to bring peace, but a sword" (Matthew 10:34), prompting Oswald Chambers to write, "Jesus Christ came to 'bring . . . a sword' through every kind of peace that is not based on a personal relationship with Himself."[16] And John Calvin said, "Peace with God is contrasted with every form of intoxicated security in the flesh."[17] Jesus was under no illusion that the world would find his peace acceptable. His followers can expect to experience trials and tribulation in the world, but ultimately the peace of Christ will prevail. "I have told you these things," Jesus said, "so that in me you may have peace. In this world you will have trouble. But take heart! I have overcome the world" (John 16:33).

The peace we long for is the Peace of God, for only his peace, "which transcends all understanding, will guard [our] hearts and [our] minds in Christ Jesus" (Philippians 4:7). This is the lasting peace that survives the pain and suffering of this life and outlasts death itself. "You will keep in perfect peace him whose mind is steadfast, because he trusts in you. Trust in the Lord forever, for the Lord, the Lord, is the Rock eternal" (Isaiah 26:3-4).

Christmas declares that *shalom* and *salvation* are dependent upon the Savior. "Today . . . a Savior has been born to you; he is Christ the Lord." Apart from the Prince of Peace, there is no salvation and there is no *shalom*. "Glory to God in the highest, and on earth peace to all on whom his favor rests." Apart from God's glory, and without God's grace, there is no peace.

"The Lord bless you and keep you;
the Lord make his face shine upon you and be gracious to you;
the Lord turn his face toward you and give you peace."
Numbers 6:24-26

CHAPTER 5

GROUND ZERO

But you, Bethlehem Ephrathah, though you are
small among the clans of Judah, out of you will
come for me one who will be ruler over Israel, whose
origins are from of old, from ancient times."
Micah 5:2

Every year, our church prepares for Christmas by offering an evening of devotional music centered on Christ called the Feast of Lights. Worship concludes with a living nativity scene made up of teenagers dressed as shepherds, older men disguised as eastern magi, and young girls playing white winged angels. For about twenty minutes, a young family in the church becomes Mary and Joseph and baby Jesus. While the congregation sings Christmas carols and electric candles are turned on throughout the sanctuary (real candles violate the fire code), all eyes are focused on the brightly lit manger scene with its costumed characters frozen for effect. The magic of this tender moment concludes with the softly sung strains of *Silent Night* and the lights are dimmed on this picture-perfect nativity scene.

That's how it happens most years; but the year I liked best was the year that Georgia Mae played baby Jesus. She screamed the entire time! Her mother tried everything to calm her, but Georgia Mae would not be pacified. Her father stood erect in shepherd garb clutching his staff and staring out into the congregation, wishing he were somewhere else. The music director was fighting to keep his concentration. He shortened the program by cutting out *O Come, O Come Emmanuel.* The incongruity of it all struck my wife as being so funny that she couldn't stop laughing. Whatever sentimentality might have been orchestrated by an eighty member choir singing softly in a candle-lit sanctuary with a living nativity scene was shattered by one little baby girl. Oh, and I should add that Georgia Mae was a perfect little angel the next evening for the second performance.

The reason I remember that evening so fondly was because I think that Georgia Mae got it right. She single-handedly threw out all of our contrived sentimentality and put everyone on edge. Nothing about Bethlehem was ever meant to be sentimental. It's always been about the mystery of God and the mess of the human condition. I doubt that Mary and Joseph would have ever said "all was calm and all was bright." It is far more likely that everyone involved was stretched to their limit. A decree from Caesar Augustus requiring everyone to register in their ancestral hometown obligated Joseph and Mary to make the five to seven day journey from Nazareth in Galilee to Bethlehem in Judea. It must not have been an easy trip for Mary, who was about to give birth to her firstborn. By the time they arrived in Bethlehem, the town was crowded and space was at a premium.

All signs point to the poverty of this couple, for when she delivered her baby, she wrapped him in strips of cloth and laid him in a manger. There is very little in either Luke or Matthew's account that suggests peace and tranquility. Mary and Joseph were conscious of being used by God and living at the center of God's great work, yet they were uprooted and alone. Whatever calm they experienced must have felt like being in the eye of the storm. They faced a strange paradox: on the one hand, they felt the power of God, and on the other, they felt powerless. According to God's sovereign plan they were in the right place, even though it was a hard place to be. Whatever feelings of nostalgia we might associate with a manger scene, we know that such feelings were not there on that first Christmas Eve.

A FALLEN PLACE

Bethlehem was not meant to be a fantasy scene in our imagination, but a real place in our history. The birth of Jesus in Bethlehem reminds us of the depravity and heartache of the human condition. The first mention of Bethlehem comes in Genesis. Jacob and Rachel were on their way to Bethlehem when Rachel gave birth to Benjamin. The delivery was difficult for her and she died shortly after delivering the baby. She named her newborn, Ben-Oni, meaning "son of my trouble," but Jacob renamed him "son of my right hand." Jacob gained a son, but lost his wife at Bethlehem. The town was remembered not as a birth place, but a burial place.

The name Bethlehem means *house of bread*, but for Naomi and her husband Elimelech it became a place of famine. Hunger forced this young family out of Judah and into Moab in search of food. When the widow Naomi returned to Bethlehem years later she was accompanied by her widowed daughter-in-law Ruth. In the town of Bethlehem, Naomi and Ruth started over. It was there that Ruth met and fell in love with Boaz, who became her kinsman redeemer. In many ways Ruth reminds us of Mary, just as Boaz reminds us of Joseph and Naomi of Anna. Ruth impresses us as sharing Mary's perspective toward God: "I am the Lord's servant. May it be to me as you have said." In Bethlehem, God did a new thing for Ruth. He took her from her pain and suffering and gave her a family. There she gave birth to a son named Obed, King David's grandfather.

God rooted his promise to the house of David, in a place so real and down-to-earth that it resists any attempt on our part to fantasize and romanticize. The town of Bethlehem was not a stage for actors but a real place for living, breathing, praying, hoping participants in God's salvation history story. Today, Bethlehem is in the news as a flash point between the Israelis and Palestinians. Through the centuries it has been the scene of continuous conflict. It epitomizes racial and ethnic conflict, and man's separation from man. Power changed hands often in Bethlehem. Recall the incident early in David's career when the Philistines occupied Bethlehem. He longed for water and said, "Oh, that someone would give me a drink of water from the well near the gate of Bethlehem" (2 Samuel 23:15). That same night, three of his men broke through enemy lines and drew water from the well near the gate of Bethlehem. Consider the irony of men having to risk their lives to get a drink of water for David from his own hometown. Such is a picture of human depravity and heroism.

Matthew's account of the birth of Christ closes with the tragic news of Herod's Bethlehem massacre. The magi escaped; having been warned in a dream not to go back to Herod, they returned to their country by another route. Joseph was warned in a dream by the angel of the Lord to flee from Bethlehem immediately. "Get up. Take the child and his mother and escape to Egypt. Stay there until I tell you, for Herod is going to search for the child to kill him" (Matthew 2:15). Herod sent soldiers to Bethlehem with orders "to kill all the boys in Bethlehem and its vicinity who were two years old and under . . ." (Matthew 2:16). Sentimentality does not stand up under the pressure of human depravity. When Matthew thought of Bethlehem, he thought of the prophecy of Jeremiah: "A voice is heard in Ramah, weeping and great mourning, Rachel weeping for her children and refusing to be comforted, because they are no more" (Matthew 2:18 from Jeremiah 31:15). Bethlehem was a place of lamentation. Think of the families that bore the grief of losing their sons because God sent his son into the world *at Bethlehem* to redeem the world. We don't like to think of the deaths of these young boys at Christmas, but they point to the cross and the death of Jesus.

Like any place, Bethlehem is a fallen place, and that's what makes it special. It is as real as where we live. God entered human history at a time and in a place that identifies fully with our situation. The great 19th century preacher Charles Spurgeon wrote, ". . . As you look at this infant, there is not the remotest appearance of temporal power. . . Here, in the cradle of the world's hope at Bethlehem, I see far more of poverty than wealth; I perceive no glitter of gold, or spangle of silver. I perceive only a poor babe, so poor, so very poor, that he is in a manger laid. . . Here, too, I see no superstition . . . there was nothing more than the stable, the straw the oxen ate, and perhaps the beasts themselves, and the child in the plainest, simplest manner, wrapped as other children are . . . no cherubs visible, no haloes."[18]

I don't think you'll ever see a painting of Bethlehem by Thomas Kinkade the highly acclaimed modern artist. Kinkade loves to paint scenes "halfway between a memory and a daydream." His first published print was an idyllic rendering of his hometown entitled *Main Street at Dusk—Placerville*. As he says, "I love to create beautiful worlds where light dances and peace reigns. I like to portray a world without the Fall."[19] It is impossible to picture Bethlehem authentically without thinking of the Fall.

A SACRED PLACE

The apostle John did not hesitate to paint a picture of Bethlehem with his Spirit-inspired words, but he found it impossible to think of Bethlehem without thinking of the reason why God came to earth and the cosmic struggle between God's grace and Satan's power.

> A great and wondrous sign appeared in heaven: a woman clothed with the sun, with the moon under her feet and a crown of twelve stars on her head. She was pregnant and cried out in pain as she was about to give birth. Then another sign appeared in heaven: an enormous red dragon with seven heads and ten horns and seven crowns on his heads. His tail swept a third of the stars out of the sky and flung them to the earth. The dragon stood in front of the woman who was about to give birth, so that he might devour her child the moment it was born. She gave birth to a son, a male child, who will rule all the nations with an iron scepter. And her child was snatched up to God and to his throne. (Revelation 12:1-5)

Bethlehem became ground zero in the drama of Salvation history. That precious moment in Bethlehem, quiet and serene, filled with wonder and worship, is nothing less than God's D-Day invasion. The beaches have been stormed. Hell threatens Heaven. The Devil shows up, not with gifts of adoration (gold, incense, and myrrh), but with strategies of annihilation (deception, treachery, and malice). Jesus' birth excites more than wonder, it excites evil. John will not allow us to be distracted from the real meaning of Christmas. God defeats the enormous red dragon with a baby, who is Christ the Lord. That is what John gives us in his nativity scene: the meaning of that moment at the manger!

The magi naturally thought that the newborn King of the Jews would be found in Jerusalem, the seat of regional power and the site of the Temple. When they came to Jerusalem, their innocent inquiries disturbed Herod and his court and prompted an emergency session with the chief priests and teachers of the law, who recited the ancient prophecy of Micah: "But you, Bethlehem, in the land of Judah, are by no means least among the rulers of Judah; for out of you will come a ruler who will be the shepherd of my people Israel" (Micah 5:2). Apparently, there was an inexplicable gap in the mind of the religious leaders between knowing this prophecy and believing in it. They were indifferent to the idea that God would actually raise up the Messiah out of Bethlehem.

What made Bethlehem so special? Throughout salvation history we observe God's resistance to man-made centers of power and so-called sacred high places. The surest way to bring down the wrath of God was to set up an idol or to designate one's own sacred place. From Aaron's Golden Calf to Herod's Temple, God resisted man-made religion. Abraham's altars were nothing more than a pile of stones. The Israelites were given strict orders not to fashion their altars into works of art, but to keep them simple and humble. An altar stood for repentance of sin and dependence upon the mercy of God. As Moses discovered in the wilderness, only Yahweh's presence could turn a place into holy ground.

Bethlehem's significance can only be attributed to the will of God. Over time it has retained its humility well. From a human point of view, it was never a very important place, but it played a significant role in salvation history. It was in Bethlehem that Samuel secretly anointed David to succeed King Saul. Bethlehem has always been an out of the way place—a humble place chosen by God to make a statement that it was not by might nor by power, but by his Spirit that the Lord would accomplish his purposes (Zechariah 4:6).

In the course of Jesus' ministry, his authority and identity were hotly debated. Some questioned, "How can the Christ come from Galilee? Does not the Scripture say that the Christ will come from David's family and from Bethlehem, the town where David lived?" (John 7:41-42). Evidently it was widely assumed that Jesus not only came from Galilee, but that he was born in Galilee. Those who knew Old Testament prophecy raised an obvious Scriptural objection. How could he be the Anointed One if he wasn't from Bethlehem? What is curious is that Jesus made no effort to set the record straight. He offered no apologetic. If there ever was a time to tell the Christmas story it certainly was then, but Jesus didn't say a word. He was not intimidated into giving an explanation to those who doubted his identity. He let his birth in Bethlehem remain a quiet truth.

Bethlehem was the right place to signify that God was fulfilling his promises. It was not a sentimental place, nor an important place, but it was the place where God chose to reveal his will in significant ways. Bethlehem symbolizes well the scandal of God's descent into human history. For it is a shocking truth. Out of the vastness of a cosmos that we cannot measure, only one small planet is known to have life. Among all the nations, cultures and civilizations on planet earth, God chose one nation, Israel, a small and relatively insignificant nation, through which to send the Incarnate One, the Messiah. Given that descent, it makes perfect sense for the birth place of the Messiah to be Bethlehem. The words are so familiar that we forget the scandal of the truth we sing.

O little town of Bethlehem, how still we see thee lie!
Above thy deep and dreamless sleep the silent stars go by.
Yet in thy dark streets shineth the everlasting Light;
the hopes and fears of all the years are met in thee tonight.

Bethlehem is the kind of birthplace you would expect for one who had to be crucified to fulfill the Father's will.

A DWELLING PLACE

The Bethlehem of salvation history, that is, the Bethlehem of Jacob and Rachel, Ruth and Naomi, Samuel and David, Matthew, Luke and John, leaves no room for sentimentality. It is a real place that inspires the celebration of the Incarnation and not a dreamlike place that celebrates infancy. It makes sense that Bethlehem, a fallen place and a sacred place, should be the right place for Jesus to be born. It is consistent with the humility of God that for the birth of Jesus, Mary and Joseph were placed by Roman edict in their crowded ancestral town sharing a room with the beasts of the field and living under the threat of Herod. Bethlehem, with its meager manger and pending doom, points to the glorious, unsentimental truth, that "the Word became flesh and lived for a while among us" (John 1:14).

It is fitting that the God who sent his son to be born in Bethlehem desires to dwell with us. Jesus used the language of birth to describe the intimacy of his indwelling relationship. Remember his words to Nicodemus, "You should not be surprised at my saying, 'You must be born again'" (John 3:7). And to his disciples he said, "Remain in me, and I will remain in you" (John 15:4). Who can grasp the humility of the risen Christ who declares, "Here I am! I stand at the door and knock. If anyone hears my voice and opens the door, I will go in and eat with him, and he with me" (Revelation 3:20)? Christ's birth in Bethlehem was completely consistent with the character of God and right in line with the humility and mystery of the Incarnation, the Crucifixion, and the indwelling of the Spirit of Christ.

O holy Child of Bethlehem, descend to us, we pray;
cast out our sin, and enter in; be born in us today.
We hear the Christmas angels the great glad tidings tell;
O come to us, abide with us, our Lord Emmanuel.

CHAPTER 6

NO ORDINARY PEOPLE

"Greetings, you who are highly favored! The Lord is with you. . . . Do not be afraid, Mary, you have found favor with God. You will be with child and give birth to a son, and you are to give him the name Jesus. He will be great and will be called the Son of the Most High. The Lord God will give him the throne of his father David, and he will reign over the house of Jacob forever; his kingdom will never end."

Luke 1:28, 30-33

The message of Christmas can be summed up in four words: *God sent his Son*. And the application of the message can be expressed in five: *the Lord is with you*. The heavenly messenger addressed these words to Mary, but they were true as well for the magi, the shepherds, Elizabeth and Zechariah, and Joseph. They are true for us. The central event of Christmas is the birth of Christ, and centered around this event is a unique gathering of people. The celebrants of the very first Christmas show us the grace of God and give us a picture of the Body of Christ. The Lord took the initiative and by his grace and love, drew the magi and the shepherds into worship. They are the true worshipers the Father seeks (John 4:23). They prove that there is a wideness in God's mercy. God broke in on Zechariah and Elizabeth and blessed and used them in ways they never imagined possible. The Lord took Mary and Joseph from obscurity and doubt and put them in the center of his will.

Compare yourself to these first celebrants of Christmas. If you are saying to yourself, "I wish God wanted to speak to me half as much as I want to hear from him," then listen closely to the Christmas message, because God wants to speak to you far more than you ever imagined. Advent reminds us of the eagerness of God to bring good news to all people. It is a message seeking a response—a celebration that inspires true worship.

Looking at these first Advent worshipers, we discover four important truths: there are no outsiders, no ordinary people, no passed-over people, and no obscure people. Together they reveal the mercy of God our Savior "who wants all people to be saved and come to a knowledge of the truth. For there is one God and one mediator between God and human beings, the man Christ Jesus, who gave himself a ransom for everyone—the testimony given in its proper time" (1 Timothy 2:3-6).

NO OUTSIDERS

To discover that there are no outsiders, we begin with the magi, those who came the furthest and arrived the latest. Matthew is arguably the most Jewish of the gospels. The first gospel account is concerned to present Jesus as King. Matthew begins with a testimony from outside of Israel that is fit for a King. "Magi from the east came to Jerusalem and asked, 'Where is the one who has been born king of the Jews? We saw his star in the east and have come to worship him" (Matthew 2:2). For the Jews, the East was a place of exile, a place of bondage and oppression. The magi came from a land of darkness and confusion. These ancient intellectuals blended science and religion, philosophy and spirituality. They were, from the Jewish perspective, the most unlikely recipients for epiphany. Yet, the Hebrew connection through generations of exiles, and with such notables as Ezekiel and Daniel, left the Scriptures in ancient Babylon to be read and pored over. Many believe that these magi came from Persia, or modern day Iraq or Iran. Think of it: ancient Iraqis among the first to acknowledge Jesus as the Messiah, the King!

Behind Matthew's stark description of the magi was an intricate understanding of prophecy and a complex arrangement of nature. During the day, they pored over Old Testament texts, and at night, they examined the sky. They made the connection between the star and ancient prophecy: "I see him, but not now; I behold him, but not near. A star will come out of Jacob; a scepter will rise out of Israel" (Numbers 24:15-17).

For Matthew, the magi are a picture of the Christian community. They represent the unexpected, but very welcome, citizens of the Kingdom of God. They are like Rahab, the surprising recipient of God's grace when the Israelites entered the promised land. They are like Naaman the Syrian, trusting in God's Word. They are like the Queen of Sheba, but they are bowing before the one greater than Solomon (Matthew 12:42). They are like the Samaritan woman in the Gospel of John and the Roman centurion in Luke's gospel. Surely if God can raise up the children of Abraham from stones, as Jesus said, then he can extend His grace to Eastern magi and Mongolians and Latin Americans. If God's grace can overcome the distance between Babylon and Bethlehem, it can overcome all cultural and intellectual barriers. As Jesus said, "I have other sheep that are not of this sheep pen . . . .there shall be one flock and one shepherd" (John 10:16).

The magi "saw the child with his mother Mary, and they bowed down and worshiped him. Then they opened their treasures and presented him with gifts of gold and of incense and of myrrh" (Matthew 2:9). In worship, the magi remind us of Melchizedek and Job, and all those who, by the grace of God, respond to what revelation they have been given. They testify to the truth of Psalm 87: "Glorious things are said of you, O city of God: I will record Rahab [Egypt] and Babylon [Baghdad] among those who acknowledge me—Philistria [Palestinians] too, and Tyre, along with Cush—and will say, 'This one was born in Zion.' Indeed, of Zion it will be said, 'This one and that one were born in her.' The Lord will write in the register of the peoples: 'This one was born in Zion.' As they make music they will sing, 'All my fountains are in you.'"

The magi affirm that the God who prepared the gospel for the world, also prepared the world for the gospel. Matthew begins and ends his gospel with the reminder that there are no outsiders."Therefore go and make disciples of all nations, baptizing them in the name of the Father and of the Son and of the Holy Spirit . . ." (Matthew 28:19). The magi remind us of that "great multitude that no one could count, from every nation, tribe, people and language, standing before the throne and in front of the Lamb" (Revelation 7:9).

NO ORDINARY PEOPLE

It is easy to identify with the shepherds because they seem so ordinary. Like the magi, they are not singled out and named. Their individuality is concealed in a group; but unlike the magi, they were not on a quest for meaning. They were just doing their job, "keeping watch over their flocks at night." The shepherds capture the most common and most innocent response to Christmas: fear, wonder, faith. "An angel of the Lord appeared to them" —unexpectedly, undeservedly, yet unmistakably! "And the glory of the Lord shone around them, and they were terrified." The canopy of a closed world of space and time is ripped apart to reveal a glimpse of the most real world. "Do not be afraid. I bring you good news of great joy that will be for all the people" (Luke 2:10).

Magi and shepherds alike received extraordinary news: the magi by studying the Scriptures and looking for God; the shepherds by being open to a revelation they couldn't ignore, "Today in the town of David a Savior has been born to you; he is Christ the Lord. This will be a sign to you: You will find a baby wrapped in strips of cloth and lying in a manger" (Luke 2:11-12). This juxtaposition of ordinary shepherds keeping watch and the heavenly host praising God and saying, "Glory to God in the highest, and on earth peace to men and women on whom his favor rests" is extraordinary. The contrast between shepherds and angels, silence and speech, fear and praise is striking. Heaven and earth do intersect! Like the shepherds, we assume we are limited to this flat land existence of "keeping watch over our flocks at night" when we are suddenly surprised by joy. We are startled into reality.

The shepherds remind us that we are all made in the image of God, and that no matter how ordinary or earthy, our souls are inscribed with God's signature. We were made to resonate with Heaven's glory. I like the way C. S. Lewis said it: "There are no ordinary people. You have never talked to a mere mortal. Nations, cultures, arts, civilizations—these are mortal, and their life is to ours as the life of a gnat. But it is immortals whom we joke with, work with, marry, snub, and exploit—immortal horrors or everlasting splendors"[20]

The shepherds' response to this startling message was just what you would have expected. "Let's go to Bethlehem and see this thing that has happened, which the Lord has told us about." So they hurried off and found Mary and Joseph and the baby, who was lying in the manger (Luke 2:15-16). Medieval Christian artists pictured the shepherds with bright haloes around their head. It was their way of saying that these are not ordinary people. Rembrandt painted shepherds with faces full of wonder, illuminated by the light of Christ.

NO PASSED-OVER PEOPLE

Elizabeth and Zechariah were the first to be brought into God's Christmas plan. They were also the oldest, the most religious, and perhaps the least expectant of God working in a new way. Those who feel their best years are behind them may identify with Elizabeth and Zechariah. They felt old and spent, but both were "upright in the sight of the Lord, observing all the Lord's commandments and regulations blamelessly." Zechariah was a priest, serving according to the age old biblical traditions. Elizabeth was barren, although she and Zechariah had prayed for years that she might have a child.

For the very first time in his long career as a priest, Zechariah entered the front part of the "holy place" in which stood the altar of incense, the golden seven-branched lampstand, and the table of show-bread. A curtain separated this front section from "the holy of holies." Only the high priest entered this rear section, and then only once a year, on the Day of Atonement. Zechariah's responsibility was simple, to clean the altar of incense and offer fresh incense. The incense served as a symbol of the prayers of the people who, as Luke informs us, were assembled outside praying. This practice had gone on for hundreds of years without incident, until Zechariah entered the holy place and the angel of the Lord appeared to him. Zechariah was "gripped with fear."

> "Do not be afraid, Zechariah; your prayer has been heard. Your wife, Elizabeth, will bear you a son, and you are to give him the name John. He will be a joy and delight to you and many will rejoice because of his birth, for he will be great in the sight of the Lord."(Luke 1:13-15)

He went into the holy place believing that he knew what God wanted from him, and he left the holy place overwhelmed with the future that God had prepared for Elizabeth and himself. Up until this point, God fit into Zechariah's expectations; after this point, Zechariah will fit into God's expectations. The promise of a son whose name would be John ("Yahweh has shown mercy"), and whose work would be to go before the Lord, was a better-than-expected fulfillment of their long-standing prayer. God's destiny for this child was way beyond their wildest dreams. He will bring back many to the Lord and he will come "in the spirit and power of Elijah, to turn the hearts of the fathers to their children and the disobedient to the wisdom of the righteous—to make ready a people prepared for the Lord" (Luke 1:17). There is a remarkable convergence of God's will and Zechariah's personal desire evident in this answered prayer. Just when Zechariah thought he must be nearing the end of his work and ministry, God was beginning a new thing.

After all these years of silence, God spoke, but Zechariah interrupted with disbelief. The angel's immediate response silenced Zechariah: "I am Gabriel. I stand in the presence of God, and I have been sent to speak to you and to tell you this good news. And now you will be silent and not able to speak until the day this happens, because you did not believe my words, which will come true at their proper time" (Luke 1:19-20). I imagine that Gabriel made a believer out of Zechariah the moment he was struck speechless. Having lost his own voice, he believed in the voice of God. When John was born, Zechariah was singing a new song and it began like this:

> "Blessed be the Lord, the God of Israel;
> he came and set his people free.
> He set the power of salvation in the center of our lives,
> and in the very house of David his servant,
> Just as he promised long ago
> through the preaching of his holy prophets . . ."
> (Luke 1:68-70, The Message)

Elizabeth and Zechariah were in the center of God's will, and their lamentation turned to celebration. Mary never expected such a wonderful, enthusiastic, Holy-Spirit greeting from Elizabeth:

> Blessed are you among women, and blessed is the child you will bear! But why am I so favored, that the mother of my Lord should come to me? As soon as the sound of your greeting reached my ears, the baby in my womb leaped for joy. Blessed is she who has believed that what the Lord has said to her will be accomplished! (Luke 1:42-45)

Like the magi and the shepherds, Elizabeth and Zechariah were surprised by joy. Even though they were old and barren, God had not passed them by, but had included them in his great work. He took their faithfulness and prayerfulness and turned it into a powerful testimony of his sovereign blessing. He brought them into the center of his great salvation history story. When I think of Elizabeth and Zechariah I think of the many I know who are older and feel physically spent, but yet have a fresh and vibrant faith in Christ. Their lives are not characterized by lamentation, but by benediction. They don't feel that God has passed them by but, on the contrary, they experience deeply the blessing of God. Like Elizabeth and Zachariah who didn't make it to the manger, they may not make it to church on Christmas Eve, but they worship Christ just as much as those who do, and continue to be a great blessing to others.

NO OBSCURE PEOPLE

The first Christmas revealed the power of God to make outsiders insiders and otherwise ordinary people into true worshipers. Those who felt passed-over were now blessed beyond expectation. We come now to Mary and Joseph who played such a prominent role in God's plan for the first Christmas. Although apart from Christ, they lived in obscurity, because of Christ they lived at the center of God's saving will. Mary's humble, hidden life was transformed by the favor of God. "Greetings, you who are highly favored! The Lord is with you" (Luke 1:28). Mary testified to this great reversal in her song of praise:

"My soul praises the Lord and my spirit rejoices in God my Savior, for he has been mindful of the humble state of his servant. From now on all generations will call me blessed, for the Mighty One has done great things for me—holy is his name" (Luke 1:46-49).

Mary went from assessing her smallness to making room in her life for God's plan and purpose. She is a model of openness to the power of God. Her life "nudges our self-centered 'me-generation' toward the path of the God-centered, the faithful, the obedient."[21] From Mary we learn about the courage to say "Yes" to God. Not only will God take up the room we give him, but God will do for us and through us what we never could have done in ourselves. It is not a matter of finding our place in this world, but of allowing God's place in our lives, for it is in this way that the proud are put down and the humble lifted up.

Joseph shared Mary's obscurity. He also shared her "Yes" to God. "Joseph, son of David, do not be afraid to take Mary home as your wife, because what is conceived in her is from the Holy Spirit. She will give birth to a son, and you are to give him the name Jesus, because he will save his people from their sins" (Matthew 1:20-21). Joseph became convinced that Mary's pregnancy was not an act of disobedience but the evidence of God at work. The Bible records no words from Joseph. "He didn't talk. He obeyed. Silently and steadfastly, he acted. He served."[22]

His faithfulness was found not in his speech, but in his obedience. He was faithful in the way that God wanted him to be faithful. Matthew says it plainly, "When Joseph woke up, he did what the angel of the Lord had commanded him and took Mary home as his wife. But he had no union with her until she gave birth to a son. And he gave him the name Jesus" (Matthew 1:24). Joseph was faithful where it counted. He was open to God's plan, even though it went well beyond his understanding. He bears silent witness, through his acceptance of Mary and her child, to God's way of establishing the household of Faith. Joseph's meekness brings the Faith down to earth. His simple acceptance of the will and word of God serves as a powerful example to us. If you like your religion to be high brow and esoteric, you had best stay away from Christianity. Joseph shows us practically and personally what it means for God to be with us.

Joseph's life illustrates well the meaning of his name, "God will add." God made room for this simple, meek man at the center of the coming Christ. The sum of his life belongs to God's credit, not his. He found his place by obeying God, which meant becoming a husband to Mary and a foster father to Jesus. It is not what we add to our lives that makes the difference for us, but what God adds to our lives.

When I think of Mary and Joseph, I think of young couples who take God at his word. The ones who are eager to fit into God's plan for their lives rather than try to fit God into their plan for their lives. They may be little in the eyes of the world, but they are highly favored in God's eyes. God lifts them up out of obscurity and puts them in his large salvation plan. Of course, God's identification with the humble goes beyond young couples and extends to all those who turn to him, from children to the elderly.

In a Nazi prison, Dietrich Bonhoeffer felt a special kinship with Mary. Shortly before he was executed he wrote an Advent poem, entitled *Where God Wants to Be.*

Where the understanding is outraged,
where human nature rebels,
where our piety keeps a nervous distance:
there, precisely there, God loves to be;
there he baffles the wisdom of the wise;
there he vexes our nature, our religious instincts.
There he wants to be, and no one can prevent him.
Only the humble believe him and rejoice
that God is free and grand,
that he works wonders where man loses heart,
that he makes splendid what is slight and lowly.
Indeed, this is the wonder of wonders,
that God loves the lowly.
'God has been mindful of the humble state of his servant.'
    God in lowliness—

that is the revolutionary, the passionate word of Advent.

CHOOSE JOY

Dave Jones surprised his daughters Madison and Hannah by putting up the family's outside Christmas lights. The girls had been out shopping, and when they returned home, to find the house decorated for Christmas, they cheered. Dave didn't feel like putting the lights up on this particular year because Dave and his wife Kathie usually did that project together. And when they finished putting up the lights they would stand across the street and look at the house. "In spite of our feelings," Dave said, "we will choose joy this Christmas."

The decision to choose joy has not been an easy one for the Jones family. They were involved in a serious car accident on Labor Day several years ago. Their car was broadsided by a fire truck. Everyone was injured, especially Kathie. Dave and Kathy, along with their oldest son Andy, were taken to Sharp Memorial Hospital. Hannah and Madison were taken to Children's Hospital. Hannah had an injured ankle. Madison had a broken pelvis and multiple lacerations. Andy suffered a severe concussion and a broken pelvis. While Dave was being checked out in the emergency room, a team of doctors and nurses were fighting to save Kathie's life. Katie, Kathie's oldest daughter, who was not involved in the accident, went back and forth between Children's Hospital and Sharp Memorial, comforting the girls and waiting for news about Kathie. Bud and Janet, Dave's parents, stayed with the girls.

That very long night in September turned into a dark night of the soul for Dave Jones and his family. Kathie's life was spared but she suffered such a severe head trauma that her brain has not recovered. In spite of fervent prayer and expert medical care, the prospect of recovery does not look good. As you can imagine, at times the fear and pain and grief have been overwhelming. When Dave says, "In spite of our feelings, we will *choose joy* this Christmas," you know that it was a difficult and painful choice. Some would say an impossible choice.

Several Christmas have come and gone and Kathie remains hospitalized in a coma. In spite of the pain, Dave continues to choose joy. He credits his sanity and his joy to Christ alone. For those of us who know him, we have seen an ordinary nice guy become Bonhoeffer in our midst. Dave has shown us the cost and joy of discipleship in ways that we never could have imagined or even dared to pray for.

* * *

Take a good, long look at the circle of worshipers gathered around Christ on that very first Christmas. The magi paying homage to the King. The shepherds "glorifying and praising God for all the things they had heard and seen" (Luke 2:20). Elizabeth and Zechariah rejoicing in the tender mercy of their God (Luke 1:78). Mary and Joseph quietly treasuring up all these things in their hearts (Luke 2:19). There's not an outsider among them. No mere mortals here, only image-bearers of God. No one is over-the-hill or all washed-up; all are alive to what God is doing. No one here is suffering from obscurity, but all are experiencing the security of God's grace and favor.

If you are an outsider, you have to have to insist on it, because God has done everything in his power to bring you home. All that can be done within the bounds of love, God has done and will do. To remain an outsider you have to become like Herod: so filled with hate and jealousy that no amount of divine revelation can penetrate. If you feel passed-over, you have to insist on it. You have to shut God out, the way the scribes and Pharisees did. Yes, you can exclude yourself from the grace and favor of God, but you have to steel yourself against every soul-resonating impulse of the gospel.

CHAPTER 7

PERFECT TIMING

*"But when the time had fully come, God sent his Son, born
of a woman, born under the law, to redeem those under
the law, that we might receive the full rights of sons."*
Galatians 4:4-5

Paul's statement sounds like a creedal confession. It is compact truth, tightly expressed, conveying in a line the mystery of the good news. The central truth is *God sent his Son,* which is modified by three concise phrases, *in the fullness of time, born of a woman, and born under the law,* followed by a purpose statement, *to redeem those under the law, that we might receive the full rights of sons* (Galatians 4:5). Indeed, Christ provides for our redemption from sin, our emancipation from slavery *and* our adoption as sons. We go from the bondage of slavery to sin to the bond of sonship with Christ. Even as God sent his son into the world to save sinners, "God sent the Spirit of his Son, into our hearts, the Spirit who calls out, 'Abba, Father.' So you are no longer a slave, but a son; and since you are a son, God has made you also an heir" (Galatians 4:6-7).

When Paul referred to sons, he was using sonship as an analogy for our status and relationship with God. My aim as a parent is to treat all three of my children as the ancients treated their firstborn sons.

Paul used the term *son* inclusively of male and female, neither excluding women nor singling out men for privilege. He made this clear when he wrote, *"You are all sons of God through faith in Christ Jesus . . ."* and then went on to say that there is neither *"male nor female, for you are all one in Christ Jesus"* (Galatians 3:26,28). So, when we quote Augustine's famous line we think inclusively: "The Son of God became the Son of Man so that the sons of men might become the sons of God."

In Greek there are two words for time, *chronos* and *kairos.* Our English word chronology comes from *chronos*. It is time measured in seconds and seasons, days and decades, months and millenniums. *Kairos,* on the other hand, is time framed by God's blessing. When *kairos* time shapes our understanding of *chronos* time we skip the Christmas re-runs and focus instead on the meaning of Advent. Repetition is replaced with Advent remembering and traditional ritual gives way to devotional worship.

Chronos describes a stream or flow of time. Nature's cycles of the earth and moon are on *chronos* time. For centuries, people told time by the sun's shadow, but it was not until the sixteenth century, when our knowledge of astronomy, geography, mathematics, and mechanics had advanced, that sundials could be marked with true hours.[23] The Egyptians may have been the first to use water clocks, devices that measured the passage of time by the amount of water that dripped from a pot. In Rome if a Senator spoke out of turn or talked too long, he colleagues would shout that his water should be taken away. To waste time was "to lose water." [24] A French monk in the eighth century is credited with inventing the sand hourglass. Teachers in England in the fifteenth century brought their hourglass to class to measure the duration of their lectures.

Mechanical timepieces began appearing in the fourteenth century. They were invented by monks who "needed to know the times for their appointed prayers. In Europe the first mechanical clocks were designed not to *show* the time but to *sound* it. The first true clocks were alarms."[25] Neil Postman, a media theorist and cultural critic at New York University, has observed that what the Benedictine monks did not foresee was that the clock is a means not merely of keeping track of the hours but also of synchronizing and controlling the actions of men.

> By the middle of the fourteenth century, the clock had moved outside the walls of the monastery, and brought a new and precise regularity to the life of the workman and the merchant. . . . The paradox, the surprise, and the wonder are that the clock was invented by men who wanted to devote themselves more rigorously to God; it ended as the technology of greatest use to men who wished to devote themselves to the accumulation of money.[26]

The monks were on *kairos* time, the merchants were on *chronos* time.

Chronos measures length of time. How many shopping days until Christmas? How long it will take you to do the Christmas cards? When is the last day you can ship packages to assure delivery in time for Christmas? *Kairos* measures meaning in time. It is a point in time that calls for action, reflection, meaning and purpose. Time can seem to stand still in a *kairos* moment. Instead of a stream of undifferentiated time, *kairos* punctuates the linear line of minutes with the pulsing heartbeat of meaning.

In the Bible, *kairos* draws attention to God's activity in salvation history. Thus, when Jesus began his public proclamation of the good news of God, he said, "The time has come. The Kingdom of God is near. Repent and believe the good news!"(Mark 1:15). When Jesus said, "The hour has come for the Son of Man to be glorified" (John 12:28), or when he said, "No one knows about that day or hour, not even the angels in heaven, nor the Son, but only the Father," he was referring to *kairos* time. God's great work had reached its climax in our space-time world and history would never be the same. *Kairos* time is "lasting time, a property of God the Creator, whereas passing time belongs to humans as creatures. *Chronos* chiefly denotes the quantitative, linear expanse of time"—years, months, days, hours, minutes. . . . But "the characteristic stress of *kairos* draws attention to the content of time"[27]

Space and time ought to humble us. The psalmist prays, "When I consider your heavens, the work of your fingers, the moon and the stars, which you have set in place, what is man that you are mindful of him, the son of man that you care for him?" (Psalm 8:3-4). If you go outside on a starry night, you gain a new appreciation for the complexity of time. Everything you see out in space is actually in the past. You've never seen a live shot of the moon or the sun. It is all "pre-recorded." Given the fact that light travels at 186,000 miles per second, our vision of the moon is delayed 1.2 seconds, our vision of the sun by eight minutes. On a clear night in the northern sky, you can see the Andromeda Galaxy. It is so far away that what we see in the present happened 2.2 million years ago. God created space and time so vast that our best scientific efforts can only serve to measure—never control—what God has made. Historian Rick Kennedy writes,

> Standing out on a rock at high altitude looking into a clear night sky,
> I sensed the complexity of time. What I see with my eyes are reports
> from millions of separate instances ranging over millions of years.
> Multiple times are registering at what is to me present time... Time
> is a wonder. It is not a line. It is not a circle. Time and distances
> shrink with acceleration and lengthen with deceleration. Speed, not
> time, is a constant in Albert Einstein's theory of relativity. Time is
> something wholly different than any analogy we use to try to describe
> it. . . . Astronomers are awash in the wildness of time. Like histori-
> ans, astronomers try to domesticate time, make it into a manageable
> model, but time refuses to be made easy. Historians and astronomers
> like to think of themselves as standing on a dock studying the sea;
> when really, there is no dock and everybody is swimming in that sea
> without a lifejacket. [28]

The vastness of space and the complexity of time rescue us from the illusion created by Rolex watches and BlackBerrys that we can somehow control time or manage it to our advantage. For a while anyway, the clock was the master metaphor of the universe. Now Daniel Boorstin says it is the master of daily life on the planet.[29] But the "mother of all machines" was replaced by the computer as the icon of the technological age. What the clock allegedly did for time, the computer supposedly does for truth, but both devices only scratch the surface of time and truth. The clock is limited to linear time and the computer is limited to binary information. Neither the clock nor the computer are very useful for interpreting the total historical process. Human ingenuity, even with the best devices, falls short in discovering the inner meaning of history. Given the vast complexity of time, observed C. S. Lewis, and the fact "that most—that nearly all history is, and will remain, wholly unknown to us," it is not a question of knowing everything it is a question "of knowing next door to nothing."[30]

Astrology was to the ancients what biology is to moderns. Until he was a Christian, Augustine looked to the stars superstitiously to determine his destiny. Astrologers told him that his actions were determined by the course of the planets. This had the advantage of removing moral responsibility and crediting one's sin to forces beyond human control. We arrive at much the same conclusion today when science claims our destiny is hardwired into our genes. Of course, science is superior to superstition and the microscope truer than the horoscope, but when the ancients looked at the stars, they were at least awed and honestly believed that there were forces beyond their control. Today, biologists tag and decode genes and expect one day soon to reconfigure our genetic makeup and control our destiny.

Historicism and scienticism share alike the conviction that the meaning and purpose of life can be discovered in an ingenious interpretation of the available facts. On the contrary, the true historian and the real scientist know this to be an illusion. Christians believe that in order to discern the fullness of time, we need not only information, but divine revelation. "History is a story with a well-defined plot," writes Lewis, "pivoted on Creation, Fall, Redemption, and Judgment. It is indeed the divine revelation *par excellence,* the revelation which includes all other revelations."[31]

PERFECT TIMING

Paul refers to *chronos* time when he speaks of the fullness of time. It is the moment in which *chronos* time is finally complete. The passing of time has reached its full measure. *Chronos* and *kairos* intersect in Jesus Christ who has given time and history a new significance.[32] With the coming of Jesus, a unique *kairos* has dawned, one by which all other time is qualified (837). The one who "was chosen before the creation of the world" has been "revealed in these last times" (*chronos*) for our sake (1 Peter 1:20). The coming of Christ becomes the reference point of all historical time, both backwards and forwards. The times of ignorance are over (Acts 17:20). The "revelation of the mystery hidden for long ages past" has been revealed in Jesus Christ (Romans 16:25).

In a few powerful lines, the early church and the apostle Paul grasped the truth of Christmas. "When the time had fully come" is not a phrase that should be passed over quickly. Meditate on the many promises of God prophetically revealed in salvation history and fulfilled in the coming of Christ. Consider the certainty of the divine promise in the time fixed by the sovereign Lord of history; reflect on the mercy of the divine patience revealed through time, beginning with Adam, continuing with Abraham and culminating in Jesus, the Messiah, the Son of David. The birth of Christ is the climax to the Old Testament's history of sacrifices and altars. He embodies the Wisdom called for in the Old Testament wisdom tradition, and he is the fulfillment of righteousness called for in the Law and the Prophets. The prophet Jeremiah proclaimed, "'The time is coming,' declares the Lord, 'when I will make a new covenant with the house of Israel and with the house of Judah'" (Jeremiah 31:31). It is this time that the apostle Paul acknowledged when he said, "In the fullness of time God sent his Son."

Some have looked at the timing of Christ's birth and reasoned that "the fullness of time" had to do with the Roman conquest. A single world government ruled from Palestine to Spain and from North Africa to southern Germany. The empire was connected by well-built roads and the Greek language. The Pax Romana was defended by Roman soldiers. Thus, the timing was right for issuing the great commission of the gospel: "Therefore go and make disciples of all nations, baptizing them in the name of the Father and of the Son and of the Holy Spirit"(Matthew 28:19).

The culture was ready. The gospel proclamation in Jerusalem was positioned to spread "to the ends of the earth" (Acts 1:8). There may be some truth to this suggestion, but I doubt if the apostle Paul was thinking about Caesar and the Roman Empire when he spoke of the fullness of time. It is more likely that he thought of the promises given to Noah and Abraham, Moses and David.

He undoubtedly thought about the roughly 1300 years that Israel had lived under the Law and the 400 years of silence since Malachi had prophesied that "the sun of righteousness will rise with healing in its wings" (Malachi 4:2). It wasn't Roman history that impressed Paul, but biblical history. "In the fullness of time" gathered up all the prophecy, promise, and passion of God's story and focused on the fulfillment of salvation history by the coming of the Incarnate One. For God "made known to us the mystery of his will according to his good pleasure, which he purposed in Christ, to be put into effect when the times will have reached their fulfillment—to bring all things in heaven and on earth together under one head, even Christ" (Ephesians 1:9-10).

Some Christians disparage the church's attention to salvation history. One church growth consultant thinks that Advent is a waste of time, because pastors are living under the illusion that they have four weeks "to tell the Christmas story," when their window of opportunity is Christmas Eve. Thomas Bandy doesn't like the idea that churches build toward Christmas, because the postmodern audience doesn't show up until Christmas Eve. He writes sarcastically,

> The church begins on the first Sunday of Advent with Advent hymns (no Christmas carols yet, please!) and somewhat obscure lectionary texts vaguely describing a coming Messiah in metaphors nobody (except presumably the church staff, some seminary professors, and random archbishops) really understands. Christmas Eve

services assume the attendees have acquired a wealth of knowledge from the past four weeks.[33]

Bandy claims Advent is a misplaced priority because

> public interest in Christmas rapidly rises to literally a fever pitch . . .
> and just as rapidly subsides into indifference . . . Give up the illusion
> that the public, and even your own church people, will give you six
> weeks to unpack the power of Christmas. But unpack you must . . .
> powerfully, experientially, and urgently . . . because time is not on
> your side.

To compensate for the culture's lack of interest in moving toward Christmas he argues that we should let go of all those obscure Old Testament lectionary texts and concentrate on the present moment power of Jesus to give people outside the church a life-changing experience. He advises preaching Colossians 1:19-20 "for every worship service throughout December, and especially on Christmas Eve." Now, I agree that this is a powerful Christmas text.

> For in him [Jesus] all *the fullness of God* was pleased to dwell, and
> through him God was pleased to reconcile to himself all things,
> whether on earth or in heaven, by making peace through the blood of
> his cross.

But how can we possibly separate *the fullness of God* from *the fullness of time?* How can we begin to understand "peace through the blood of his cross" apart from the valuable revelation that led up to the birth of Christ? We cannot lift Jesus out of salvation history and treat him as a present moment phenomenon that can somehow give people a spiritual experience on Christmas Eve.

He is right about the fever pitch, the holiday spin, and the postmodern impatience with "the fullness of time," and also, that the churches are filled with strangers on Christmas Eve. It's true some of these strangers will be very open to the gospel, but many will be cynical and skeptical, and some, simply tired shoppers. But all of them will need to hear the

Christmas message, and none of them will ever be offered a greater gift than the gift of God through Jesus Christ our Lord. It is not our desire to obscure the gospel of God's grace in any way; we only seek to lift up the fullness of the gospel for all to embrace. But, for the sake of commending the gospel to a lost generation, it is better to dwell on the patience of God than to fixate on the impatience of postmodern people.

NOW IS THE TIME

Many may be surprised to learn that *the fullness of time* arrived nearly eighteen hundred years before Immanuel Kant declared *man had come of age* and Thomas Paine celebrated his *age of reason*. Long before the Age of the Discoverers, the Enlightenment, the Industrial Revolution, the Scientific Age and the Computer Age, the apostle Paul confessed, "in the fullness of time God sent his Son. . ." This is why he declared, "I tell you, now is the time of God's favor, now is the day of salvation" (2 Corinthians 6:2). Secularists argue that the modern age came about because people stopped believing in God, but secularism ignores the historical fact that the Christian worldview inspired the exploration of the world and the investigation of a rational universe. Christianity played a key role in the transition from astrology to astronomy, from magic to medicine, from superstition to science, from aristocracy to democracy, and from poverty to industry. We forget that Christians founded universities and hospitals, fought for emancipation, and carried the gospel to the ends of the earth. It is not so surprising that the fullness of time should have taken place when it did, because so much of what has followed in history is related to the coming of Christ.

Modern notions of mistrust and skepticism, combined with the arrogance that glories in "the ascent of man," make it difficult for many to believe that our present happiness and eternal destiny depends on the Incarnation of God. Our personal histories cannot be separated from the life, death and resurrection of the historical Jesus. Christians believe that everyone has a story, but only one story redeems our story. God's Salvation History is vital to the meaning and fulfillment of our own personal story. We arrive at that conclusion not by human ingenuity and scientific proof, but by the revelation of God.

History in its totality is too broad for us to comprehend and interpret but the history of redemption, as it is revealed by God's Spirit through human testimony is close enough for us to understand and believe. Only twenty or so people in succession separate us from the eyewitnesses to Jesus' resurrection. My grandfather was born in 1881 and lived for 93 years on earth. He was twenty people removed from living in the first century. Wendell Berry, in his novel *Jayber Crow*, has Jayber, an aging village barber, reminisce:

> History grows shorter. I remember old men who remembered the Civil War. I have in my mind word-of-mouth memories more than a hundred years old. It is only twenty hundred years since the birth of Christ. Fifteen or twenty memories such as mine would reach all the way back to the halo-light in the manger at Bethlehem. So few rememberers could sit down together in a small room.[34]

"Our modern schools do much to undermine the closeness of history," writes Professor Kennedy. "Our history textbooks encourage us to think of ourselves as separated from the past. We are taught to assume the past to be a foreign and exotic place. A vast distance is supposed to exist between us and the eyewitnesses to the resurrection. Trusting the reported events in the New Testament is considered a leap of faith, something risky, possibly unreasonable. But Jayber Crow is right. A small room of people is all that is needed to link us personally to the eyewitnesses. No leap is necessary. . . . As Christians founded upon the historical fact of the resurrection of Jesus, we only need twenty or so conscientious people linked through time to give us the confidence of listening to the eyewitnesses. And to give us greater confidence, we have written attestations that have been passed along to keep the testimony on track."[35]

We observe Advent not to keep a tradition, but to grow in the grace and knowledge of our Lord Jesus Christ. The church through the ages, which need not be longer than 20 people in succession, has encouraged Christians to arrive at Christmas prepared devotionally, with a sense of joy and wonder peaked by personal contemplation and worship. We set aside this time each year to focus on God's wonderful gift, and we celebrate the birth of Christ. For those who follow the Lord Jesus, there is a profound sense of wonder and joy at the mystery of the Incarnation of God and the meaning of eternal redemption in Christ. How we live in the present depends on how we understand "the fullness of time." When people turn their attention away from "fullness of time" and say, in effect, "Let's just enjoy the day we have," they run into trouble, because "the day we have is never understood, and certainly not appreciated, on its own terms. It always exists as part of a greater whole."[36] And the greater whole can only be understood in the light of the coming of Christ; because Christ came "in the fullness of time" our time has meaning, purpose, significance and fulfillment.

CHAPTER 8

GOD SENT HIS SON

*"But when the time had fully come, God sent his Son, born
of a woman, born under the law, to redeem those under
the law, that we might receive the full rights of sons."*
Galatians 4:4-5

God invaded the mess of the human condition in the most personal and costly way imaginable. Into our crisis of sin and death, God sent his own Son "in the likeness of sinful man to be a sin offering" (Romans 8:3). Christmas celebrates God's love for us. "This is how God showed his love among us: He sent his one and only Son into the world that we might live through him. This is love: not that we loved God, but that he loved us and sent his Son as an atoning sacrifice for our sins" (1 John 4:9-10).

Sentimentality is just as much a foe of the true Christmas message as the Holiday Spin Cycle. If we need to distinguish between *chronos* and *kairos*, we should also distinguish between sentiment and love. For many, Christmas is a decorative season, defined more by a holiday mood than the meaning of salvation and devotion to God. Sentimentality looks to feelings to inspire faith; love looks to faith to inspire feelings. Over the years, we are tempted to develop traditions that burden ourselves and the season with a demanding to-do-list. Love is not just a cozy feeling. Love calls for action, embracing the other person in some significant way.

We respond to God's movement towards us. We are able to "draw near to God with a sincere heart in full assurance of faith," because God has taken the initiative and drawn near to us in Christ (Heb 10:22). We are able to show love to others because of the love of Christ in our lives. The wisdom of God knows "that we can *act* ourselves into a new way of feeling much quicker than we can *feel* ourselves into a new way of acting. Worship is an *act* which develops feelings for God, not a *feeling* for God which is expressed in an act of worship."[37]

Sentimentality can rule the ritual of the season. I know a woman who goes to great effort and expense every year to decorate every room of her large, beautiful home. Each room is transformed for the holiday season into something that could be proudly displayed in the holiday issue of *Better Homes and Gardens*. And every year the same circle of friends is invited to her home for the holiday tour so they can ooh and ah over her wonderful decorations.

When I think of impressive Christmas decorations, my mind goes back to the Christmas I spent in Myer Memorial Hospital in Buffalo, New York. I was recovering from cancer surgery. That was the year that Bill Richardson, my best friend in high school, did something very unexpected. My parents and I were more in a survival mode than a holiday mood and my brother had gone to visit grandparents in Wisconsin. My hospital room consisted of World War 1 vintage furniture and a bare light bulb hanging from the ceiling. Bill was upset that I was in the hospital over Christmas, but from my perspective, it was one hard year out of the many years of great Christmases. Bill's life was much more difficult than mine. His parents had gone through a difficult divorce and he didn't get along with his father's new wife and step-sisters. I wasn't sure Bill could remember the last time he had a fun Christmas. Then, a few days before Christmas, Bill surprised us all by showing up at my hospital room with a four-foot high Christmas tree. He bought the tree, the lights and the decorations at the department store where he worked after school. He set the tree up in the corner of the room, strung the lights and decorated it.

And everyone who came into my room commented on Bill's Christmas tree—I mean, everyone! Of course, my greatest joy in all of that was not the decorated Christmas tree, but being able to tell everyone about my friend Bill.

THE SENDING GOD INVADES

"Enemy-occupied territory—that is what this world is," writes C. S. Lewis. "Christianity is the story of how the rightful king has landed, you might say landed in disguise, and is calling us all to take part in a great campaign of sabotage."[38]

The sending of his Son is the climax to a coherent history of costly commitments. When God said to Abraham, "Leave your country, your people and your father's household and go to the land I will show you," he set in motion a modus operandi that reach its fulfillment in the sending of his Son (Genesis 12:1). God's future intentions become even more ominous when he said to Abraham, "Take your son, your only son Isaac, whom you love, and go to the region of Moriah. Sacrifice him there as a burnt offering on one of the mountains I will tell you about" (Genesis 22:2). Abraham's words to Isaac resound through the centuries: "God himself will provide a lamb for the burnt offering, my son" (22:8), and God did, but the event points forward to the sending of God's own Son. And the Lord's commendation of Abraham hints of the greater gift to come, "Now I know that you fear God, because you have not withheld from me your son, your only son" (22:12). We cannot help but be reminded of the apostle John's testimony: "For God so loved the world that he gave his one and only Son that whosoever believes in him should not die but have everlasting life" (John 3:16).

Before Abraham, there was Job. Job illustrates the extent to which God will go to gain the victory over evil. Job offers us a very early reason for the Cross and a picture of Christ as the Suffering Servant. God sends Job into the battle with Satan to prove that faithfulness to God and the righteousness of God is stronger than evil. But the big question is, "Where is God in all this pain and suffering?" Is God the divine bystander, the outside observer, the ultimate regulator making sure that the balance between order and chaos is maintained? God's answer is more personal and sacrificial than we could have imagined. His response to our pain and suffering climaxes in the sending of his Son. God puts himself into the battle with evil and suffers not only with us, but for us. God fights for our salvation not as we might expect, swooping down and destroying all opposition, but by taking upon himself the judgment of our sin. God himself dies on the Cross for our sins, and with His atonement comes victory over suffering and death. Christ, the Lamb that was slain before the creation of the world, sent by God.

There is nothing sentimental about God sending his son to be sacrificed for our sins. In place of a red-coated jolly Santa picture Isaiah's Suffering Servant—the One sent by God:

> He had no beauty or majesty to attract us to him, nothing in his appearance that we should desire him. He was despised and rejected by men, a man of sorrows, and familiar with suffering. Like one from whom men hide their faces he was despised, and we esteemed him not. (Isaiah 53:2-3)

The coming of Jesus Christ is the invasion that all of history has been longing for. It is the missing part that brings everything into perspective. C. S. Lewis offers a helpful analogy:

> Let us suppose we possess parts of a novel or a symphony. Someone now brings us a newly discovered piece of manuscript and says, 'This is the missing part of the work. This is the chapter on which the whole plot of the novel really turned. This is the main theme of the symphony.' Our business would be to see whether the new passage, if admitted to the central place which the discoverer claimed for it, did actually illuminate all the parts we had already seen and 'pull them together.'[39]

LOVE IN MOTION

The Father's love, given in the sending of his one and only Son, is far from sentimental but it is inherently emotional. Originally, emotion referred to movement rather than feelings. It meant to move out, migrate, to transfer from one place to another. It came to mean a stirring in one's heart or a feeling of agitation, but its early meaning meant physical action and actual movement. Emotion was defined more by action than feeling—more by movement than mood. "To love someone is to move your life toward them and to leave the former position in which you were settled as an isolated individual."[40] In love, God made the first move toward us and has continued the movement ever since. The emotion we experience toward God is based on his grace-filled movement towards us. To discover the meaning of Christmas emotionally, rather than sentimentally, means "moving closer to God who in Jesus Christ left the preferred place of heaven to move toward us."[41]

Jesus was well aware of the Father's love and the part he served in putting this love in motion. With that in mind he told an Advent parable that sentimentalists everywhere try hard to ignore (Matthew 21:33-46). Once, *there was a landowner who planted a vineyard.* The imagery of a vineyard immediately recalls Isaiah's song of the vineyard (Isaiah 5:1-7) and the history of God's loving care. The landowner walls off his vineyard, builds a winepress and a watchtower, and trustingly rents it out to some farmers. When the harvest season comes, and Jesus uses the word *kairos* to distinguish this special moment, the landowner sends three servants to collect the rent. But the tenants are inherently and ruthlessly evil. They beat up one servant, kill another and stone a third. This three-fold rejection advertises the tenants' blatant and deliberate disregard for the landowner's authority over his property and his investment in their success. Nevertheless, the landowner sends out a second and even larger team of servants, but they are treated the same way. *Last of all, he sent his son to them. 'They will respect my son,' he said.* Surely to the world, it is the landowner who looks hopelessly naive, a sentimentalist if there ever was one. Someone has defined failure as the ability to make the same mistake twice and expect a different result. But to be fair to the landowner, the whole moral order is on his side. There is no debate here as to whose cause is just and right. The landowner's investment in his vineyard is now beyond calculation.

We are not surprised to learn that the tenants killed the son. *So they took him and threw him out of the vineyard and killed him.* But what is shocking and absurd is that they think that by killing the son they will receive his inheritance, as if the landowner is going to somehow disappear. Do they think that he lives so far away that he will never bother with them? Don't they realize that he has sent his son! Jesus posed the rhetorical question: *Therefore, when the owner of the vineyard comes, what will he do to those tenants?* Unknowingly, the crowd hearing Jesus' story is heading to the same end as the wicked tenants. They are in the process of rejecting Jesus, the Son sent by God, just as they had rejected the prophets who came before him. The logic of the story leads inevitably to judgment for those who kill the Son. The crowd understands the logic of the story, but not the point of the parable. They give their verdict, *He will bring those wretches to a wretched end and he will rent the vineyard to other tenants, who give him his share of the crop at harvest time (kairos).*

Several years ago, International Justice Mission (IJM) learned from local aid workers that an especially heinous form of sexual exploitation was taking place in Svay Pak a remote village eleven kilometers from Phnom Penh in Cambodia. After prayer and careful consideration, IJM sent in undercover investigators who captured images of little girls as young as seven and eight being sold by pimps to be raped or molested by western pedophiles. IJM presented detailed evidence to the Cambodian authorities who repeatedly failed to respond because of a complex web of deception, open bribery, and payoffs to the police.

Gary Haugen, President of IJM, writes, "There was a point of reckoning where I knew we must act—for true love requires action. The lawless and brutal are fully dedicated to their work and those who oppose them must operate with even greater commitment. So together we lay the enormity of the problem at the feet of the God who moves mountains and cried to the Maker of these innocent ones. We began crafting a strategy to get these girls out and to bring the perpetrators to account."[42]

Prayerfully and painstakingly, IJM sought the help of high-level officials in Cambodia, the U.S. government and colleagues in the human rights field. It took professional excellence, political savvy, raw courage, and daily dependence upon God to move the case forward. Sharon Cohn, Director of Anti-Trafficking Operations, writes, "I poured my heart out to God and asked for wisdom to move the U.S. Embassy to act on the girl's behalf. As I described to the Ambassador and his staff what was happening to these children and what we wanted to do, I realized that perhaps God had created me just for this moment. Soon, we got the word that the Deputy Prime Minister of Cambodia had ordered his people to work with us to get these girls out."

After much prayer and painstaking preparation, IJM moved in with eighty Cambodian police officers and rescued thirty-seven girls and arrested thirteen perpetrators. IJM has extended God's hand of grace to these children who have suffered so greatly and has sought safe and loving homes for each one of the girls. The Love of God sent IJM to rescue these girls, even as God sent his Son to rescue us from sin and death. We are like those young girls in need of salvation.

It is easy to celebrate the *mood* of Christmas without Jesus. Many do. But it is impossible to celebrate the *meaning* of Christmas without Jesus. Sentiment defines Christmas as Santa Claus and evergreen trees, Rudolph and mistletoe, shopping and gifts. Love defines Christmas as God sending his Son. Dietrich Bonhoeffer drew a telling analogy between his incarceration and the Incarnation: "A prison cell, in which one waits, hopes, does various unessential things, and is completely dependent on the fact that the door of freedom has to be opened *from the outside*, is not a bad picture of Advent." The freedom we long for and the salvation we seek comes *not* from within, but from Jesus who came that we may have life, and have it to the full (John 10:10).

CHAPTER 9

BORN OF A WOMAN

*"But when the time had fully come, God sent his Son, born
of a woman, born under the law, to redeem those under
the law, that we might receive the full rights of sons."*

Galatians 4:4-5

In the third phrase of this confessional statement, the apostle Paul
focuses on the reality of the humanity of Jesus. This is a qualifying
phrase that modifies the central truth of the confession that "God sent
his Son." The sending God invaded his own space/time creation *in
person*. In the fullness of time, history's stream of linear *chronos* time
was intersected by God's grace-filled *kairos* time. The Incarnation of
God was a one time event in real time at just the right time for all time.
The "image of the invisible God," "the firstborn over all creation," was
sent by God, who "was pleased to have all his fullness dwell in him,"
in order "to reconcile to himself all things, whether things on earth
or things in heaven, by making peace through his blood, shed on the
cross" (Colossians 1:15-20). Each phrase in the apostle Paul's confession
is an affirmation of the down-to-earth, heaven-revealed reality of the
Incarnation of God.

FACT AND FICTION

To many it seems far-fetched to believe what is actually said about heavenly visitations and the miraculous conception of Jesus. Martin Luther once remarked that the Incarnation consists of three miracles: "The first, that God became man; the second, that a virgin was a mother; and the third, that the human heart should believe this." Luke was concerned to lay out the evidence to convince a skeptical Greek audience that what was said about Jesus was true. He begins his account by drawing on eyewitness testimony and conducting a careful investigation into everything from the beginning. He did this to reassure the recipient of his account, Theophilus, of "the certainty of the things you have been taught."

It doesn't take a literary genius to realize the difference between myth-making and history-writing. The accounts of the birth of Christ are not sentimentalized or embellished. On the contrary, there is an austerity about the factual narrative that describes reality as it is beheld by eyewitnesses and personal participants. Everything depends upon the truth of the Incarnation. Luke's account does not read, "Once upon a time . . ."; it reads, "Today in the town of David a Savior has been born to you; he is Christ the Lord" (Luke 2:11). The apostle John said it well, when he said,

> That which was from the beginning, which we have heard, which
> we have seen with our eyes, which we have looked at and our hands
> have touched—this we proclaim concerning the Word of life. The life
> appeared; we have seen it and testify to it, and we proclaim to you the
> eternal life, which was from the Father and has appeared to us. We
> proclaim to you what we have seen and heard, so that you also may
> have fellowship with us. (1 John 1:1-3)

How we begin to tell the Christmas story is especially important. Most people begin Christmas with fiction. Judging from one of the local mega bookstores, when it comes to Christmas, people are reading just about everything else but the true Christmas story. Of the more than fifty titles on the special Christmas book display, there was only one that was about Christ. All the rest were homey, holiday tales and murder mysteries, such as *Deck the Halls with Murder* and *Silent Night: Stories of Romance and Suspense*. I had no idea that Christmas murder mysteries were so popular. Several titles caught my eye: *The Physics of Christmas: From the Aerodynamics of Reindeer to the Thermodynamics of Turkey*, *Deck the Halls with Buddy Holly* and *Lighten Up, It's Christmas!* Most of the books on display were in the human interest category, stories about angels, long-lost relatives, and foster children; in addition a collection of books on Santa, such as *Santa: My Life and Times*, *Santa and Pete*, and a copy of *Believe in Santa Treasury*. I suppose it should not surprise us that there were more books on Santa than about Jesus on the Christmas book display.

One year, J. Sidlow Baxter, a well-known pastor, sampled what various preachers had to say about Christmas. "To one, Christmas was a symbol of intangible aspirations. To another, it was an idealistic enshrinement of motherhood and family life. To another it was 'the most significant domestic festival in the Church's calendar.' But when I turned back again to our Lord's own explanation," Baxter writes, "this is what I found: 'The Son of Man came not to be served, but to serve, and to give his life as a ransom for many' (Matthew 20:28). If *anyone* knows, 'the reason why,'" Baxter emphasized, "*He* does. His is the one explanation of Christmas that really matters."

Ironically, the more we add to Jesus' own explanation, the more inadequate our understanding will be. Baxter said it well: "In view of our Lord's words, it is intolerably inadequate to offer some beautifully worded yet merely aesthetic explanation of Christmas. Our Lord's incarnation was not merely idealistic; it was redemptive . . . Bethlehem and Golgotha, the Manger and the Cross, the birth and the death, must always be seen together if the real Christmas is to survive with all its profound inspirations; for 'the Son of Man came not to be served, but to serve, and to give his life a ransom for many'."[43]

THE MIRACLE OF BIRTH AND THE GRAND MIRACLE

There is nothing like the birth of a child to make a mockery of the belief in nature alone. When I stood in the delivery room and held our seven-pound newborn, I was overwhelmed by the sheer glory of her. The birth of a child causes us to reexamine the meaning of life, to contemplate God's sovereignty, and to feel our dependence upon God.

Some who doubt the virgin birth wonder why more is not made of it in the Bible. Reference to the virgin birth is found only in Matthew and Luke. Mark and John make no mention of it and the book of Acts is silent about this miracle of conception. The virgin birth is missing from Peter's sermons and Paul's evangelism; nothing is said about it in the earliest confessions. As far as we know, the virgin birth was not a well-publicized theological concern until Ignatius of Antioch (writing about A.D.110) emphasized it in his apologetics against those who denied the humanity of Jesus. Explicit mention is made, of course, in the Apostle's Creed: "I believe in God the Father almighty, creator of heaven and earth; And in Jesus Christ, His only Son, our Lord, who was conceived by the Holy Spirit, born from the Virgin Mary . . ."

Roman Catholicism, in particular, has responded to this biblical reserve by elaborating and inflating the significance of the virgin birth. Roman Catholics have traditionally spoken of "the threefold virginity of Mary": the virginal conception, the virginal birth and perpetual virginity of Mary. But the Bible is careful to limit the miracle to the conception of Jesus; everything else, including the pregnancy and birth, is otherwise completely normal.

That the Bible is reserved about the virgin birth should not cause us to doubt the miracle. This same reserve is true of all Christ's miracles. The real issue in the gospels and epistles was not the means God used in the Incarnation, but the fact of the Incarnation. "If the thing happened," writes C. S. Lewis, "it was the central event in the history of the Earth—the very thing that the whole story has been about. Since it happened only once, it is by Hume's standards infinitely improbable. But then the whole history of the Earth has also only happened once; is it therefore incredible?"[44]

The issue is not so much *how* God came to occupy Mary's womb as much as it is *why*. The nature of the miracle was never meant to obscure or overwhelm the identity of the One conceived. The question is whether the miracle of the Incarnation of God is consistent with what we know of God through the nature of his creation and the working out of his salvation history. Lewis reasons that the Incarnation fits with the fact that God created us as "composite" beings. We are "a faint image of the Divine Incarnation itself—the same theme in a minor key."[45] We know ourselves to be more than DNA. The "nature alone" world view does not account for the reality we live with everyday.

He also sees a movement within Creation that is consistent with the Incarnation. Within the nature of creation itself there is a kind of built-in sympathy or love that moves downward in order to raise creation upward, like the strong man stooping down to help a small child.

> We can understand that if God so descends into a human spirit, and human spirit so descends into Nature, that our thoughts into our senses and passions, and if adult minds (but only the best of them) can descend into sympathy with children, and humans into sympathy with animals, then everything hangs together and the total reality, both Natural and Supernatural, in which we are living is more multifariously and subtly harmonious than we had suspected. We catch sight of a new key principle—the power of the Higher, just in so far as it is truly Higher, to come down, the power of the greater to include the less.[46]

The reasonableness of the Incarnation is evident not only in the nature of creation but in the character of salvation history. God chose a small, insignificant people through whom to bless all people. The scandal of particularity narrows salvation's means down to a specificity that seems incredible, yet perfectly consistent with everything else about creation and redemption

> Out of enormous space a very small portion is occupied by matter at all. Of all the stars, perhaps very few, perhaps only one, have planets. Of the planets in our own system probably only one supports organic life. In the transmission of organic life, countless seeds and spermatozoa are emitted: some few are selected for the distinction of fertility. Among species only one is rational. Within that species only a few attain excellence of beauty, strength, or intelligence.[47]

When it comes to redemption, the selectiveness of God is not based on merit, but mercy. The covenant of love is not extended to the best and the brightest, but to the smallest and the weakest (Deuteronomy 7:7-9). But God does not play favorites. "The 'chosen' people are chosen not for their own sake (certainly not for their own honor or pleasure) but for the sake of the unchosen. Abraham is told that 'in his seed' (the chosen nation) 'all nations will be blest.' That nation has been chosen to bear a heavy burden. Their sufferings are great: but, as Isaiah recognized, their sufferings heal others."[48]

Added to this principle of *Selectiveness* or *Divine Prerogative* is the principle of *Vicariousness* or *Divine Prerequisite*. There is plenty of advanced intelligence (warning) in the history of redemption that alerts us to the fact that God is going to enter into the dilemma of the human condition *personally*. Job's experience implies it. Abraham's near sacrifice of Isaac suggests it. Isaiah's prophecy of the Suffering Servant spells it out, and David's lament cries out for it. Vicariousness is built into the whole sacrificial system. By the time Jesus came, we should have expected it. "The Sinless Man suffers for the sinful, and, in their degree, all good men for all bad men."[49] It is these characteristics of creation and redemption, the composite nature of the person, the pattern of descent, the selectiveness of God in choosing a planet and choosing a people, and the vicariousness in God's sacrificial system that all point to the reasonableness of the Incarnation of God.

The early church gave considerable thought as to how best to express the meaning of the Incarnation. The Chalcedonian Creed (451 A.D.) confessed that our Lord Jesus Christ is "truly God and truly man . . . like us in all things except without sin; begotten from the Virgin Mary, the Mother of God, as regards his manhood; one and the same Christ, Son, Lord, only-begotten, made known in two natures without confusion, without change, without division, without separation . . ." They affirmed that Jesus, the Incarnate One, was born of a woman.

Inspired by the Holy Spirit, the author of Hebrews may have put it best when he wrote, "Since the children have flesh and blood, he too shared in their humanity so that by his death he might destroy him who holds the power of death. . . ." (Hebrews 2:14). Moreover, "we do not have a high priest who is unable to sympathize with our weaknesses, but we have one who has been tempted in every way, just as we are—yet was without sin" (Hebrews 4:15). So it can be said of Jesus, the Son of God, that he "learned obedience from what he suffered and once made perfect, he became the source of eternal salvation for all who obey him. . ." (Hebrews 5:8-9).

THE MOTHER OF JESUS

Mary was a real flesh and blood human being, not a symbol or a paradigm or an icon. She is not a literary figure nor a fictional character, she is one of us. She is not the mediator between God and humanity as some have made her out to be, but she is the mother of the one mediator between God and all people, "the man Christ Jesus, who gave himself as a ransom for all" (1 Timothy 2:5). Mary is our first example of how we should respond to the Incarnation of God, and we can learn a great deal from her—Jesus' first disciple.

Mary is a model of openness to the power of God. "Not only was she a simple mortal, unpretentious enough for us all to identify with, but she nudges our self-centered 'me generation' toward the path of the God-centered, the faithful, the obedient. If we read Mary into each one of the Beatitudes, we will not falsify her character."[50] Mary accepts the word of the Lord to her. The angel said to her, "Greetings, you who are highly favored! The Lord is with you." This blessing would stay with her for the rest of her life, "the sound and the meaning of it would live and throb in Mary's mind as a perpetual sign of God's affirmation and approval, in spite of all the trials that would track her life."[51]

Luke tells us that "Mary was greatly troubled at [the angel's] words and wondered what kind of greeting this might be. But the angel said to her, 'Do not be afraid, Mary, you have found favor with God. You will be with child and give birth to a son, and you are to give him the name Jesus." When we hear this story today, it seems to be all about credibility; but for Mary it was about courage, taking God at his word, saying "yes" to God. She teaches us the first rule of discipleship: to find our lives we need to lose our lives in the will of God. We see this wonderful, joyous coming together of Mary's life and God's plan; this convergence of micro prayers and God's macro will.

Mary asked the right question: "How will this be, since I am a virgin?" On the surface it seems unfair that Zechariah should have been silenced for his question and Mary honored and reassured for hers. Their questions sound similar. The difference between, "How can I be sure of this?" and "How can this be since I am a virgin?" may not seem great, but it was great! For Zechariah it was a question of God proving himself; for Mary it was a question of God overcoming her limitations. Zechariah should have known better. His familiarity with the Word of God and its promises for Israel's future should have prevailed over his own skepticism. Instead of imposing his own skepticism upon God, he should have been open to God fulfilling his revealed promises. Mary simply and sincerely needed to know more. Her question was neither skeptical nor cynical. She questioned her ability to fulfill God's will. The difference between Zechariah and Mary is the difference between skepticism and humility. Zechariah questioned the ability of God to fulfill his promise; Mary questioned her ability to live up to God's desire for her.

Mary embraces the will of God and gives us the best definition of discipleship when she says, "I am the Lord's servant. May it be to me as you have said." We rejoice with Mary, who was the first to welcome Christ into her life. "My spirit rejoices in God my savior." We are surprised by Mary's self-understanding, her capacity to understand herself in the light of God's mercy. We are impressed by her God-centeredness, her focus on "the Mighty One" who has done great things for her. We are awed by her grasp of salvation history, her ability to see God's hand at work. "She stands at the head of a long line of saved sinners, justified by faith alone through Christ alone."[52]

The extraordinary thing that Mary did was to make room for God. The God of creation, Maker of heaven and earth, invited her participation in the most personal way possible. I appreciate the way Canadian hymn writer, Margaret Clarkson, describes this occupancy:

Lord of the universe, Hope of the world, Lord of the limitless
reaches of space, here on this planet you put on our flesh, vastness
confined in the womb of a maid: born in our likeness you ransomed
our race: Savior, we worship you, praise and adore; help us to honor
you more and yet more! [53]

The vastness of God confined in the womb of Mary was accomplished by divine initiative and human submission. Mary's response to the call of God was, "May it be to me as you have said." We confess that making room for God is not how we look at life. Typically, we wonder if there is any place in this world for us. "Where do I fit in?" is the normal response, especially among young people. "How can I find my place in this vast, competitive, confusing world?" The circumstances of life seem to conspire against us. Most of the time we feel unrecognized, unnoticed and anonymous. It's like we don't belong here, and when we are noticed, it seems like we are put down or embarrassed. Mary's life reminds us that the real issue in life, for her as well as for us, is not finding our place in this world, but of making room in our lives for God.

BORN AGAIN

Yong Lee is a good friend who came to Christ while studying medicine at UC Berkeley. It was there that he first became aware of a dilemma in his soul—a dilemma captured by Richard Holloway, an episcopalian minister:

*This is my dilemma. I am dust and ashes-frail, wayward, a
set of predetermined behavior or responses. Riddled with fears,
beset with need, the quintessence of dust and unto dust I shall
return. But there is something else about me. Dust I may be,
but troubled dust. Dust that dreams. Dust that has strange
premonitions of transfiguration, of the glory in store, a destiny
prepared, an inheritance that will someday be my own. So my
life is stretched out in a painful dialectic between ashes and
glory, between weakness and transfiguration. I am a riddle to*

myself, an exasperating enigma, this strange duality of dust and glory.

At UC Berkeley, Yong became aware of his status as *troubled dust.* There, in an exquisitely diverse marketplace of ideas, he found himself at the crossroads of this dualism. Stimulated by a curious, as well as, skeptical mind, he embarked on a personal journey which he hoped would lead to his coming of age as a man.

Three things happened in close succession: first, the death of a classmate, which raised questions about his own significance; second, his study of science and his empirical observation of human anatomy and physiology, which produced in him a sense of fascination and awe; and third, a disappointing Psychology class that limited the study of the human person to observing behavior.

One night, after finishing his reviews for the Winter finals, Yong took a long stroll and gazed at the night sky. For the first time in his life, the trajectory of the stars and the grandness of the cosmos overwhelmed him. Looking at the orderliness of this cosmic spectacle, he felt a strange presence around him. It was as if someone was trying to communicate with him. It was so real that he had to go home and tell his family about it. Predictably, they thought that their worst fears had been realized and that Yong had become a victim of Cal's academic pressures.

Yong began to study religion and philosophy. He read many western thinkers, including Sartre, Bertrand Russell, and Camus, as well as eastern thinkers, such as Confucious and Lao Tze. He talked with Buddhist monks and Christians. It became clear to him that a purely rational, scientific view of the world was not enough. We have a natural intuition that treasures the realm of the imagination, that allows us to see poetry as more than ink on a piece of paper, or a sunset as more than tricky refraction of light through the atmosphere, or even the kiss of lovers as simply the joining of two sets of lips. The very rules of logic, which are immaterial, insist on the existence of a higher dimension.

On the other hand, residing in a world of fantasy and superstition aside from known scientific facts would be disastrous escapism. Real imagination and wonder require an attachment to our true physical nature. Yong recalls a conversation with an oncologist at Beth Israel, who insisted that faith was incompatible with reason. Yong responded by saying that faith in God was not the defeat of reason, but the recognition that reason is restricted in what it can know about the world.

> Rationality and careful decision making can only take us so far.
> There must also be a holy sense of imagination, delight, and love
> that accompanies our reason, and in the end takes us further
> than the limits of reason. This is what Chesterton meant when
> he claimed, 'Poets do not go mad; but chess-players do. . . . The
> madman is not the man who has lost his reason. The madman is
> the man who has lost everything except his reason.[54]

In reading the Gospel of John, Yong came to the conviction that John was presenting Jesus as God's coherent thinking in human form. God's reason and wonder came together in the Word that was made flesh and dwelt among us and we beheld his glory full of grace and truth.

It makes sense. The God who sent his son to be born in Bethlehem desires to dwell with us. Jesus used the language of birth to describe the intimacy of this indwelling relationship. Remember his words to Nicodemus, "You should not be surprised at my saying, 'You must be born again'" (John 3:7). And to his disciples he said, "Remain in me, and I will remain in you" (John 15:4). Who can grasp the humility of the risen Christ who declares, "Here I am! I stand at the door and knock. If anyone hears my voice and opens the door, I will go in and eat with him, and he with me" (Revelation 3:20)? Christ's birth in Bethlehem was completely consistent with the character of God and right in line with the humility and mystery of the Incarnation, the Crucifixion, and the indwelling of the Spirit of Christ. The indwelling reality of Christ in you is surely a miracle on the order of the virgin conceiving the Incarnation of God.

CHAPTER 10

BORN UNDER THE LAW

*"But when the time had fully come, God sent his Son, born
of a woman, born under the law, to redeem those under
the law, that we might receive the full rights of sons."*
Galatians 4:4-5

Each of these descriptive phrases moves us closer to the purpose of
the Incarnation of God. Each has a depth of meaning difficult to
fathom. We are led from the big picture of salvation history ("in the
fullness of time") to the greatest movement of love known to humanity
("God sent his Son"). Our confession moves us from "In the beginning
was the Word, and the Word was with God, and the Word was God" to
"the Word became flesh and made his dwelling among us" (John 1:1,14).
Then, the confession narrows down and focuses our attention: first, on
the particular means God used to fulfill his will with the phrase "born
of a woman"; and second, on God's specific purpose: "born under the
law to redeem those under the law." It is impossible to over-estimate
the density of truth packed into this little phrase. All that is meant by
righteousness and justice, reconciliation and redemption, is subsumed
in the phrase *under the law.*

The law of God does not seem to fit with the holiday mood, and it
certainly is a foreign concept in your typical Christmas letter. Every

year we get this great letter from friends in California. Compared to everyone else who sends us Christmas letters they blow the competition away. They go to more exotic places and do more fun things than all of our friends combined. They have more fun in one year than I have had in my lifetime. They live in a 5,000 square foot mansion and have a beautiful lakehouse, but they love to travel, down to Mexico in February to play with the whales and over to New York for a Broadway play in April. In May, the wife travels to Ireland for her own personal time away and then the family spends three weeks in Australia, visiting the outback, befriending an Aboriginal community, diving off the Great Barrier Reef, crocodile hunting on the Daintree River, and attending an opera at the Sydney Opera House. Their sons are excellent athletes, certified in SCUBA diving, accomplished musicians, and leaders of their church youth group. In addition to his law practice, the husband plays piano in a jazz band and loves it.

Now, I ask you, where in the midst of all that excitement does the law of God come in? Who is going to break in on all that fun and say,

> There is no one righteous, not even one; there is no one who under-
> stands, no one who seeks God. All have turned away, they have
> together become worthless; there is no one who does good, not even
> one. . . .Now we know that whatever the law says, it says to those who
> are under the law, so that every mouth may be silenced and the whole
> world held accountable to God. Therefore no one will be declared
> righteous in his sight by observing the law, rather, through the law we
> become conscious of sin. (Romans 3:10-20)

THE LAW AND THE CHRISTMAS STORY

Everyone in the Christmas story lived under the law and they took it to heart. It was God's revelation. To them the law was not an authoritarian task master, but a special life-transforming, character-shaping word from God. The educated heart shares God's deep aspirations for justice and righteousness and applies these convictions to ordinary life. Life is placed in orbit around a quality of being that reflects spiritual devotion, ethical discernment, and a teachable spirit. Zechariah was a priest under the law and his wife Elizabeth was a descendant of Aaron. "Both of them were upright in the sight of God, observing all the Lord's commandments and regulations blamelessly" (Luke 1:6). They shared the psalmist's love for the law: "I will walk in freedom, for I have sought your precepts" (Psalm 119:45). "Your promises have been thoroughly tested, and your servant loves them" (Psalm 119:140).

We may not give a lot of thought to the role of the law in the Christmas story, but Joseph did. He was the first to feel the tension between law and gospel. Mary's concern had to do with the laws of nature, but Joseph's consternation had to do with the moral law. He was well aware of what the law said about sexual fidelity and when he learned that Mary was pregnant he decided to divorce her quietly. When Matthew refers to "divorce," he does not mean that Joseph and Mary were already married. In that culture, to be pledged to be married meant that separation was much more than breaking off an engagement. Matthew tells us that Joseph "was a righteous man and did not want to expose her to public disgrace" (Matthew 1:19). By divorcing Mary quietly he sought to spare her the shame and disgrace of publicly exposing her unfaithfulness, even as he sought to save himself from disobeying the law by marrying a woman who now belonged to someone else. Under the law, Joseph's strategy would not only have satisfied his conscience, but shown compassion to Mary. And this is the action he would have taken if the angel of the Lord had not spoken to him in a dream, saying, "Joseph son of David, do not be afraid to take Mary home as your wife, because what is conceived in her is from the Holy Spirit. She will give birth to a son, and you will give him the name Jesus, because he will save his people from their sins" (Matthew 1:20-21).

Two things can be said about the law in Joseph's case: first, the law complicated life and second, the law was inadequate to save. Nevertheless, Joseph would have found living under the law a blessing, not a burden. He rejoiced in the law and would have agreed with the Psalmist when he said, "The law of the Lord is perfect, reviving the soul" (Psalm 19:7).

Mary's song of praise reflects a world-view based on the law of God. The Magnificat is more than lyrical poetry, it is a carefully crafted unified field theory of theology and ethics based on the law of God. Mary has a firm grasp of the reality of God and salvation history. She speaks of "God my Savior" who is "mindful of the humble state of his servant." He is "the Mighty One," master of everything, whose "mercy extends to those who fear him, from generation to generation." This is the God of Abraham, "Holy is his name." He scatters the proud, lifts up the humble, fills the hungry with good things and sends the rich away empty. Clearly, these are not the musings of a flighty, self-absorbed teenager, but the song of a woman of God shaped by the law of God.

What Mary and Joseph did after Jesus was born is another indication of how seriously they took the law. Jesus was circumcised on the eighth day according to the law, and after Mary's forty day purification, he was presented to the Lord as their consecrated firstborn son. They offered a sacrifice "in keeping with what is said in the Law of the Lord: 'a pair of doves or two young pigeons'" (Luke 2:22-24). In the Jerusalem temple Mary and Joseph were received by Simeon, who is described as "righteous and devout." He took the baby Jesus into his arms and praised God, saying, ". . .My eyes have seen your salvation, which you have prepared in the sight of all people, a light of revelation to the Gentiles and for glory to your people Israel" (Luke 2:31-32). Simeon, along with the 84-year-old prophetess Anna, saw in Jesus the coming Redeemer. All of this to say that the law of God shaped the character of everyone in the Christmas story, and more importantly, framed their understanding of the meaning and purpose of Jesus' birth.

THE PURPOSE OF THE LAW

Everything that is contained in the biblical concept of the law is encompassed in this defining statement. From the beginning humanity has been under the law. In the garden, Adam and Eve were under the law. A limit was set that served to define the difference between themselves and God, between the creature and their Creator. "The balance of things is seen in the contrast between 'every tree' that is there for human enjoyment and the single tree that is forbidden. Yet in that single tree was enshrined the principle of law."[55] Since we are made in the image of God, our humanity is most fully realized in obedience to the will of God. In other words, we are truly ourselves when we live in accordance with the will of God. A fully human life is an obedient life, for it is only when we live according to the perfect law of liberty that we become free (Psalm 119:45; James 1:25). Sin is a violation of the will of God and an attack on our true nature.

The full impact of the law came at Mount Sinai after the Passover, a sign of God's promised redemption, and after the Exodus, Israel's liberation from bondage. "The people redeemed by blood were brought by their Redeemer to the place of lawgiving (Exodus 20:2). Grace precedes law; the law of God is not a system of merit whereby the unsaved seek to earn divine favor but a pattern of life given by the Redeemer to the redeemed so that they might know how to live for his good pleasure."[56] The Mosaic Law gave Israel a legal system to guide their administration, a moral code to guide holy living, and a ceremonial law to guide true worship. It is important to emphasize that the precepts, statutes, and commands of the law were based on redemption and rooted in a sacrificial system. It was never about rules and human merit. It was always about a way of life made possible by the grace of God. The precepts were rooted in a theology of propitiation and the statutes were based on an atoning sacrifice. Human obedience has always rested on Divine forgiveness. No one was ever meant to imagine that there was salvation in a law that was independent of God's grace and redemption.

The temptation we face is to live by a code of conduct rather than to live by the grace of God. We are egotistically inclined to believe in our own merit rather than to trust in God's mercy. Sadly, we prefer to rely on our own judgment than to follow God's will. So, we are tempted to think that we are good enough, if we try hard enough. This is why the holiday season is such a burden to so many, because it seems that it is all about trying harder, when in fact, Christmas is all about receiving the gift of salvation in Christ.

In Romans, the apostle Paul spells out the value of the law, but only after he makes clear that the law did not give the Jews bragging rights on their relationship with God. The Gentiles had the law, too, "since they show that the requirements of the law are written on their hearts, their consciences also bearing witness, and their thoughts now accusing, now even defending them" (Romans 2:15). If the Jews were "entrusted with the very words of God" it was not for the purpose of showing preferential treatment, much less righteous merit, but to show that "all have sinned and fallen short of the glory of God" (Romans 3:2, 23). The purpose of the law, Paul insisted, was "so that every mouth may be silenced and the whole world held accountable to God. Therefore no one will be declared righteous in [God's] sight by observing the law; rather, through the law we become conscious of sin" (Romans 3:19-20).

My best friend in middle school was Ron Goldstein. I can't remember how we became friends, but we did. Our families seemed very different. Ron's father dressed in expensive suits, drove a black Cadillac and owned a night club that had a dubious reputation in town. It was definitely not the kind of place my parents went to. But Ron was a good friend and we spent a lot time together. He was Jewish and when he turned 13 he invited me to his bar mitzvah. Having reached the age of accountability, he was to be designated a "son of the law" and formally "yoked to the law." From then on, it was his responsibility to obey the law.

It was the first time I had ever been to a synagogue. The solemn ceremony involved unfurling a large scroll, the Torah, from which Ron was called upon to read briefly in Hebrew. "Hear, O Israel: The Lord our God, the Lord is one. Love the Lord your God with all your heart and with all your soul and with all your strength. These commandments that I give you today are to be upon your hearts" (Deuteronomy 6:4-6). I knew he had worked hard to get the pronunciation correct. The large gathering of extended family, the giving of expensive gifts, and a formal meal made it feel like a wedding. I was really impressed that Ron received all this attention for turning thirteen. After the meal, the immediate family and close friends went back to Ron's home. Then something happened that gave the day a different perspective for me. There were seven or eight of us, Ron's cousins and friends, upstairs in his room, laughing and joking around, when Ron's brother came in with a three foot stack of pornographic magazines. He unceremoniously dropped the stack in the middle of the room letting the glossy magazines slide in all directions. It produced an instantaneous feeding frenzy. My friend, Ron, who a few hours earlier had been ceremonially designated a "son of the law" was reduced to a drooling puppy, ogling the centerfolds. As I walked home, I tried to sort out the incongruity of this rite of passage in my mind. Paul was right. We are not saved by the law, but "through the law we become conscious of sin."

The law was put in charge, Paul said, "to lead us to Christ that we might be justified by faith" (Galatians 3:24). Righteousness is not a competition to see who can keep the law. If it were, everyone would lose, because everyone falls short of the glory of God. We are all powerless to meet God's standard. Some of us may seem more powerless than others, but we are all powerless! This is why Jesus said "unless your righteousness surpasses that of the Pharisees and the teachers of the law, you will certainly not enter the kingdom of heaven" (Matthew 5:20). Jesus did not simply set the law aside or ignore it. He fulfilled it. As he said, "Do not think that I have come to abolish the Law or the Prophets; I have not come to abolish them but to fulfill them" (Matthew 5:17). To fulfill the law, Jesus not only kept the law perfectly—the only person to do so— but he stood in our place and received the punishment that we deserve for not keeping the law. The author of Hebrews wrote, "For we do not have a high priest who is unable to sympathize with our weaknesses, but we have one who has been tempted in every way, just as we are—yet was without sin" (Hebrews 4:15). Righteousness is not a competition; it is a gift! Because "God made him [Jesus Christ] who had no sin to be sin for us, so that in him we might become the righteousness of God" (2 Corinthians 5:21).

Singing Christmas carols more for their meaning than their melody, makes us conscious of our sin and our need for redemption. The carols are sung sweetly and with a familiar lilt, but their message is serious and their meaning critical. They are more like battle hymns against sin and death than sentimental carols. They identify the Savior and define the purpose of the Incarnation of God.

Come, thou long-expected Jesus, born to set thy people free; from our fears and sins release us; let us find our rest in thee.

The carol asks, *What child is this* who lays *in such mean estate?* The reason given is anything but gentle: *for sinners here the silent Word is pleading. Nails, spear shall pierce him through, the cross be borne for me, for you. . . . This, this is Christ the King. . . . King of kings salvation brings.*

Silent Night! awaits *the dawn of redeeming grace* and O Holy Night sings, *long lay the world in sin and error pining, till he appeared and the soul felt its worth.* In hushed tones we sing, *I wonder as I wander, out under the sky, how Jesus the Savior did come for to die* and in Hark the Herald Angels Sing, we proclaim triumphantly *God and sinners reconciled!*

These anthems of adoration keep the redemptive purpose of Christ's coming in clear view.

The source of *Joy to the World* is not in doubt, because *the Lord has come! No more let sins and sorrows grow, nor thorns infest the ground; he comes to make his blessings flow far as the curse is found, far as the curse is found, far as the curse is found.*

UNDER THE LAW OR IN CHRIST

Several Christmases ago, my family went all out to surprise me with an incredible gift. Around Thanksgiving, Virginia and Kennerly picked out a seven week old Golden Retriever puppy. The breeder was a wonderful Christian woman who truly loves dogs and cares for them well. They left the puppy with its mother for a couple of weeks and conspired as to how they were going to pull off this surprise. Since my family knows that I tend to be preoccupied through Advent, they decided that this was a gift that would have to wait for Christmas morning. They picked up the puppy about a week before Christmas and friends volunteered to keep it at their home. Meanwhile, I had absolutely no idea of what had excitedly preoccupied the minds of my family for almost a month.

On Christmas morning, when I drove downtown to pick up my mother, Kennerly got the puppy and hid him so I wouldn't see him when we returned home. We all opened our gifts like we normally do, and then I was told to close my eyes because I had one more surprise. So, I closed my eyes and seconds later a warm, ten-week old puppy was dropped into my lap. I was shocked. Virginia said I turned white. In the moment, I couldn't recall ever having asked for a puppy, but there he was, an adorable, wide-eyed Golden Retriever who looked up at me quizzically. We named him Frodo.

I'm getting a little old for these kind of surprises, but it was a wonderful Christmas present, and it had all the features of a family story that will be told for years to come. The whole experience evoked the kinds of feelings we associate with a great family Christmas. Then, the week after Christmas, Virginia took Frodo to the vet for a second set of shots and came home in tears. The vet listened to Frodo's heart and said, "I'm sorry to tell you this, but this dog's heart could stop at any time. It has a serious defect. If I were you, I'd take the dog back to the breeder and ask for your money back." Virginia and Kennerly were crushed and so was the breeder. The breeder's vet checked Frodo out and came to the same conclusion. The puppy didn't have long to live.

The Frodo experience is a parable for me that fits the Christmas season well. Try as we might to get around the harsh realities of life, Christmas only seems to accentuate them, not deny them. We knock ourselves out trying to please our loved ones. We shop until we drop, send out cards, decorate our homes, sing carols, travel great distances to be together, and dress up in red. But thankfully, Christians can't forget the purpose of the Incarnation of God. The Bible will not cooperate with Bing Crosby's "I'm Dreaming of a White Christmas." "Jingle Bells! Jingle Bells! Santa's on his way" doesn't hold a candle to "Joy to the World, the Lord has come, let earth receive her King." The Holiday Spin Cycle is optional, but the meaning of Christmas is not. Our lives depend on Christ for time and eternity. Only Jesus can bring us home. The Holy One is our Redemption and our Righteousness. To God be the glory!

In Christ alone who took on flesh
Fullness of God in helpless Babe
This gift of love and righteousness
Scorned by the ones He came to save
'Til on that cross as Jesus died
The wrath of God was satisfied
For ev'ry sin on Him was laid
Here in the death of Christ I live

In Christ Alone, K. Getty & S. Townend

CHAPTER 11

COMING HOME
FOR CHRISTMAS

". . .God sent the Spirit of his Son into our hearts,
the Spirit who calls out, "Abba, Father."
Galatians 4:6

We can't escape the longing for home, a longing that seems especially strong at Christmas. We visualize that first Christmas and imagine great relational tenderness between Mary and Joseph and a true sense of reverence among the shepherds. There is a quiet suspense that captures our imagination. We are caught up in a drama bigger than ourselves. We know that the conditions were primitive and the circumstances were difficult, but we have a profound sense of the meaning and intimacy in that family picture. Mary wrapped the Christ child in strips of cloth and laid him in a manger. God wrapped his birth in prophecy and promise, and we want to be wrapped up into this family picture created by the triune God, Father, Son, and Holy Spirit. Most nativity scenes include the magi, even though it appears that they came sometime later. Like the magi, we want to get in on the experience.

LONGING FOR HOME

For me, Christmas Eve is always a highpoint for that feeling. I want to be wrapped up in the reality of the Incarnation of God. Some Christmases when I was growing up, we would brave the winter weather and drive the twelve hour trip from Buffalo, NY, to Racine, Wisconsin to be with Grandpa and Grandma Haumersen. Christmas day was a family reunion that barely fit in my Grandparents' home. There were twenty-six of us including aunts, uncles and cousins. I remember the piles of Christmas presents and feeling way too excited to eat. Other years we stayed at home. The Christmas Eve that I played a shepherd in the Christmas pageant at church was not especially enjoyable. I was way too nervous and I got tired of trying to stand still. But what I appreciated the most were those years that we spent Christmas Eve together as a family—just the four of us. My brother and I would turn all the lights off except for the Christmas tree lights. My mother fixed hot chocolate. We sang a few Christmas carols quietly. And Dad read the Christmas story in Luke 2 and prayed.

Into our crisis of sin and death, God sent his own Son "in the likeness of sinful man to be a sin offering" (Romans 8:3). Christmas celebrates God's love for us. "This is how God showed his love among us: He sent his one and only Son into the world that we might live through him. This is love: not that we loved God, but that he loved us and sent his Son as an atoning sacrifice for our sins" (1 John 4:9-10). In love, God made the first move toward us and has continued the movement ever since. The emotion we experience toward God is based on his grace-filled movement towards us. For us to discover the meaning of Christmas emotionally, rather than sentimentally, means "moving closer to God who in Jesus Christ left the preferred place of heaven to move toward us."[57] He left his home to bring us home.

> *Thou didst leave Thy throne and Thy kingly crown*
> *When Thou camest to earth for me;*
> *But in Bethlehem's home was there found no room*
> *For Thy holy nativity. . . .*

THE HOLY NATIVITY

The Holy Nativity is an extraordinary moment, filled with wonder and grace; but it is also a picture of hardship and humility. "In the fullness of time," came at a most inopportune time and "God sent his Son" into the poorest of conditions. Mary and Joseph were not only under God's law, but the law of the land, and just as Mary is about to go into labor, they were required to leave their home in Nazareth for a seven-day journey to Bethlehem. They were not at home in their ancestral home and there was no room for them in the inn. Jesus was laid in a borrowed manger. So, while the reality was anything but homey, the nativity makes us think of our true home, which is really not a place at all, but our family in Christ.

For Mary and Joseph home was not an idyllic setting. Home was being together at the center of God's will. If we think of home as the wonderful place where we grew up or the painful place that we left in disgust, we will think of the Holy Nativity as someone else's family, but not our own.

Searching for our true home in God is made difficult by living in a society that tries to dismantle any connection between heaven and earth. It is a society of restless nomads looking for a little heaven on earth, defining their identity by appearances, insisting on relationships that meet their needs, and then wondering why they suffer from loneliness. Absorbed in their own life stories, they miss the opportunities to become involved in the greater drama of God's salvation history. In striving to change their own lives, they cannot be converted by the gospel.[58]

Many restless nomads have grown accustomed to an endless search without any expectation of finding their true home. They find many small truths in many places, but no central truth to guide their vision of life. They tell themselves that Christmas Eve inspires sentimental feelings rooted in tradition, rather than the quest of the soul, moved by the Spirit of God and born of truth. It is easy for them to dismiss the meaning of the Holy Nativity by blaming it on the mood. They confuse a warm cozy feeling for the end of the matter. But what if those feelings are not the end of the matter but a fresh stirring of the soul that longs for a true home?

Before we left Toronto, I wanted to show Jeremiah and Andrew where I grew up (Kennerly was too young to make the trip). So we drove from Toronto to Buffalo, stopping off at Niagara Falls to take some pictures. I wanted the boys to see my roots. We visited my parents' first home in Hamburg, New York, and then we visited the cemetery where my father was buried in Orchard Park. He went to be with the Lord at the age of 49. The boys posed by his memorial stone. It read,

DONALD D. WEBSTER - WITH CHRIST - 1923-1972.

Jeremiah and Andrew were good sports that day. We took pictures of my elementary school and high school and our old house in Williamsville.

I'm glad we took that one-day journey because it convinced me, somewhat unexpectedly, of two truths. First, home is not so much a place as a family. It is far more personal than an old house or past memories, even though the place and the memories may be very good. The boys, typical for their age, were not impressed by my old houses and schools. I realized in their company that I wasn't very impressed with the houses and the schools either.

The second lesson I learned was that my home is not where I'm from, but where I'm going. I had no desire to return to my roots or to live in the past. I am caught up in a relational story that moves forward with the motion of God's love. I haven't arrived. "I press on to take hold of that for which Christ Jesus took hold of me" (Philippians 3:12).

I realize that for many, Christmas is a painful reminder of what they didn't have when they were growing up; for me, it holds memories of growing up in a loving home. But that is not enough. No matter how loving and caring our families may be, the search for home will never be satisfied by our immediate family. What we need is to be adopted into God's family. We are born with an identity that does not fulfill us, and that is why we never find our real home until we are at peace with God.

Your spouse cannot be your savior, nor can your children be your future. You can try to make them your salvation, but I can tell you right now, that will not work. There is something more than your individual self and the people that please you. There is a deeper, more abiding relationship that you were created for that gives meaning and purpose to all other relationships.

BORN IN ADAM, ADOPTED IN CHRIST

We all were born in Adam and we all were meant to be adopted in Christ. Our sons, Andrew and Jeremiah, remind me of what it is like to be adopted in Christ. There was no greater joy than when Virginia and I adopted them. Andrew was born hundreds of miles away, but in seven days he was at home with us. Our daughter, Kennerly, helps me to see that there is no difference in a father's heart between the child who is adopted and the child who is conceived.

I have always thought it appropriate that our oldest son's biological mother gave him the name Adam. He bore that name officially for only a few days, but we all bear that name historically as an identifying condition. We may not be *called* Adam, but we are *in* Adam. "For as in Adam all die, so in Christ all will be made alive" (1 Corinthians 15:22). That may seem far removed from anything you feel about yourself, but your identity in Adam is as true as your DNA or blood type or the color of your eyes. "Like Adam," Frederick Buechner writes, "we all lost Paradise; and yet we carry Paradise around inside of us in the form of a longing for, almost a memory of, a blessedness that is no more, or the dream of a blessedness that may someday be again."

In addition to nurturing his physical life for nine months in her womb, Jeremiah's biological mother left him a five-page typewritten letter. The adoption agency suggested that we wait to show him this letter until Jeremiah showed a mature curiosity about his birth parents. From the beginning we talked about adoption with Jeremiah and Andrew. We were eager to express to them what a miracle and blessing they are to us, but we held off showing Jeremiah the letter. Then, one day, when he was going through some files in the hall closet, he came across a file labeled "Jeremiah." He removed the file from the cabinet and opened it expecting to find report cards and immunization records, but instead he discovered a letter, which began, "At the time I am writing this letter you have just been born."

Alone with the letter, he felt like he was facing part of his past that had always been an illusion. Jeremiah was always imaginative. He fantasized that his "real" parents were probably multi-millionaires living in a castle in London eating pizza and chocolate ice cream for dinner every night. He claims this explains why he ran away from home often. Picking up his room, cleaning the bathroom, feeding his fish—in the mind of an eight-year-old these were burdens equivalent to a labor camp. I went off in search of my son several times, but he had never gotten very far, and always seemed happy to return home.

The letter gave Jeremiah a picture into his past that, up until then, had been shaped by his imagination. It explained that his parents were college students studying literature at university. The letter offered a detailed list of attributes, pet peeves, descriptions of where they lived, and even an account of the weather at the time the letter was being written. Finally, in the last paragraph, she explained *why*. They had struggled throughout their relationship with personality conflicts that eventually led to their breakup. She wanted her son to have a better life than the one she could provide. Jeremiah was impressed with her selflessness and how much love it took for her to give up her child.

Like Jeremiah at eight years old, we are prone to childish fantasizing about our past. We forget that we are in Adam and that our birth family is inadequate to meet our needs. It is easy for us to cultivate the little dreams that keep us preoccupied and distracted from our need for redemption. But "when we allow the story of our lives to be rooted in a story greater than ourselves, we are not limited to the small life that we can construct for ourselves."[59] "The first man Adam became a living being; the last Adam, a life-giving spirit" (1 Corinthians 15:45).

In the Gospel of John, we read, "He was in the world, and though the world was made through him, the world did not recognize him. He came to that which was his own, but his own did not receive him." For any number of reasons, people fail to recognize who Jesus Christ is. But that need not be said of you or me. We have heard the truth proclaimed. We have had every opportunity to respond to Christ and to belong to his family. It is not just an emotional response or a sentimental reflex, receiving Christ is our primary relationship, more real than any other relationship we could possibly have. "Yet all who received him, to those who believed in his name, he gave the right to become children of God—born not of natural descent nor of human decision or a husband's will, but born of God" (John 1:10-13).

On Christmas we celebrate being adopted into the family of the Everlasting Father. We celebrate not only Christ's birth, but our new birth in Christ. We thank the Lord for coming into the world *and* coming into our lives. We are not fatherless, cosmic orphans, estranged from the most meaningful relationship possible, but in Christ we are the true sons and daughters of God. As the apostle wrote, ". . . God sent the Spirit of his Son into our hearts, the Spirit who calls out, 'Abba, Father'." So we are no longer slaves but his children and heirs of Christ (Galatians 4:4-7). The meaning of Christmas brings us to our knees and causes us to thank the Lord for his indescribable gift.

NOTES

1.   Dietrich Bonhoeffer, *Letters & Papers From Prison* (New York: Macmillan, 1972), 133.

2.   J. Countryman, *Rembrandt: The Christmas Story* (Nashville: Thomas Nelson, 1998), 9.

3.   Margaret Clarkson, *A Communion Hymn for Christmas.*

4.   Michael Kelly, "The white-light, colored-light debate," *San Diego Union Tribune,* January 12, 2001.

5.   M. Craig Barnes, *Sacred Thirst: Meeting God in the desert of our longings* (Grand Rapids, MI: Zondervan, 2001), 87.

6.   Stephen Nissenbaum, *The Battle for Christmas* (New York: Vintage Books, 1996), 7.

7.   Ibid., 9.

8.   Ibid., 8

9.   Ibid., 48.

10.   Ibid., 173.

11.   Ibid., 177.

12.   Stuart Briscoe, *Meet Him in the Manger* (Wheaton, IL: Harold Shaw Publishers, 1996), 22-23.

13.   R. E. O. White, "Salvation," in *Evangelical Dictionary of Theology,* ed. Walter A. Elwell (Grand Rapids: Baker, 1984), 968.

14.   Charles Colson, *Kingdoms in Conflict* (New York: Morrow, 1987), 370.

15.   J. Alec Motyer, *The Prophecy of Isaiah* (Downers Grove, IL: IVP, 1993), 103.

16.   Oswald Chambers, *My Utmost for His Highest,* Dec.19.

17.   Quoted in Karl Barth, *Dogmatics in Outline* (New York: Harper, 1959), 151.

18.   Charles H. Spurgeon, *12 Christmas Sermons* (Grand Rapids: Baker, 1994), 76-77.

19.   Randall Balmer, "The Kinkade Crusade," *Christianity Today*, Dec. 4, 2000, 51.

20.   C. S. Lewis, *The Weight of Glory* (New York: Collier, 1965), 19.

21.   Luci Shaw, "Yes to Shame and Glory," *Christianity Today*, Dec. 12, 1986, 22.

22.   Walter Wanegrin, A Stranger in Joseph's House, *Christianity Today*, Dec. 11, 1995, 17.

23.   Boorstin, *The Discoverers* (New York: Vintage, 1985), 27.

24. Ibid., 32.

25. Ibid., 36.

26.   Neil Postman, *Technopoly* (New York: Knopf, 1992), 14-15.

27.   J. Guhrt, *Dictionary of New Testament Theology*, vol. 3 (Grand Rapids: Zondervan, 1978), 826.

28.   Rick Kennedy, *Jesus, History, and Mt. Darwin: An Academic Excursion*, (Eugene, OR: Wipf and Stock, forthcoming).

29.   Boorstin, 72.

30.   C. S. Lewis, *Christian Reflections* (Grand Rapids: Eerdmans, 1967), 107.

31.   Ibid., 103.

32.   H. C. Hann, *Dictionary of New Testament Theology*, vol. 3 (Grand Rapids: Zondervan, 1978), 843.

33.   Thomas Bandy, "This is the Christ Postmodern People Need to Hear About," *NETResults*, Nov/Dec 2000, 13-14.

34.   Wendell Berry, in his novel *Jayber Crow* (Berkeley, CA: Counterpoint Press, 2001).

35.   Kennedy, "Remembering the Resurrection," *Modern Reformation* 13:2, March/April, 2004, 40-42, 47.

36.   Craig Barnes, *Searching for Home* (Grand Rapids: Brazos, 2003), 79.

37.   Eugene Peterson, *A Long Obedience in the Same Direction* (Downers Grove: IVP, 1980), 50.

38.   C. S. Lewis, *Mere Christianity* (Collier, 1960, 46.

39.   C. S. Lewis, *Miracles* (New York: Macmillan, 1947), 115.

40.   Barnes, *Searching for Home* (Grand Rapids: Brazos, 2003), 159.

41. Barnes, 160.

42.   Gary Haugen, Cambodia Special Report, 2003, International Justice Mission.

43.   J. Sidlow Baxter, *Awake My Heart* (Grand Rapids: Zondervan, 1960), 371.

44. Lewis, *Miracles*, 112.

45.   Ibid., 115.

46.   Ibid., 115.

47.   Ibid., 121.

48.   Ibid., 122.

49.   Ibid., 122.

50. Luci Shaw, "Yes to Shame and Glory," *Christianity Today*, Dec. 12/1986, 22.

51. Shaw, 22.

52. David Neff, "Let Mary Be," *Christianity Today*, Dec. 8, 1997, 15.

53. Margaret Clarkson, "Lord of the Universe," *Hymns II*, ed. Paul Beckwith, Hughes Huffman, Mark Hunt (Downers Grove: IL, 1977), 176.

54. Craig Barnes, *Searching for Home*, 131.

55. J. A. Motyer, "Law," *Evangelical Dictionary of Theology* (Grand Rapids: Baker, 1984), 623.

56. Ibid, 624.

57. Barnes, *Searching for Home*, 160.

58. Ibid., 69.

59. Ibid., 67.

12.95

Printed in the United States
200209BV00006B/1-249/A